TILE
style

PATTERN
GUIDE

TILE *style*

PATTERN GUIDE

A comprehensive
color-by-color directory
for decorating with
tiles, plus room-by-room
inspirational examples

JILL BLAKE

KNICKERBOCKER
PRESS

A QUARTO BOOK

First published in
North America in 1996 by
Knickerbocker Press
276 Fifth Avenue, Suite 206
New York, NY 10001

A catalogue record for this book is
available from the British Library.

ISBN 1-57715-006-6

This book was designed and produced by
Quarto Publishing plc
The Old Brewery
6 Blundell Street
London N7 9BH

Senior editor Michelle Pickering
Senior art editor Catherine Shearman
Copy editors Barbara Cheney, Maggie
McCormick
Designer Roger Daniels
Illustrators Pippa Howes, Elizabeth Gray,
Keren Querfurth
Tile collages Mary Fellows
Photographers Martin Norris, Les Weiss,
Richard Gleed
Picture researchers Miriam Hyman,
Lizi Freeman, Jill Taylor
Picture manager Giulia Hetherington
Art director Moira Clinch
Editorial director Mark Dartford

Typeset in Great Britain by
Central Southern Typesetters, Eastbourne
Manufactured in Malaysia by
CH Colour Scan Sdn Bhd
Printed in Singapore by
Star Standard Industries (Pte) Ltd

CONTENTS

INTRODUCTION

Tiles, in various shapes and forms, and made from a variety of natural materials – from clay and cement to stone, marble and slate – have been both a decorative and practical building material for as long as humans have created shelters in which to live and designed specific places of beauty in which to worship a deity.

We all know of the mosaic or tesselated pavements which graced the temples, foyers, forums and houses of the ancient Romans. Many can still be seen today in sites all over Europe – they may well have been walked on for over two thousand years! But as excavations have shown, tiles were used by many other early civilizations – ancient Egyptian, Persian (Iranian), Babylonian, Moorish, Arabian, Mongol, Islamic, Chinese, Japanese – to add color, pattern, richness and sophistication to floors and walls.

In medieval times, churches, cathedrals, cloisters and monasteries often had decorative flagged or tiled floors, the patterns of which are still as fresh and colorful today as when they were laid more than six hundred years ago. In the seventeenth and eighteenth centuries, as a result of travels made by the members of the East India Company in search of furniture, fabrics and artifacts to import and sell in Europe, the decorations of Chinese porcelain began to influence those of tiles. Tin-glazed tiles in rich colors (known as Majolica tiles) became very popular, and the Dutch developed a thriving tile industry in the seventeenth century to supply the ever-increasing demands throughout Europe. They also developed their own designs, using simple hand-painted motifs of flowers, flowerpots, tulips, animals, peasant figures and rustic scenes. Blue and white became more popular than the brighter colors, and both the motifs and the blue and white coloring has become synonymous with Dutch Delftware.

In the nineteenth century in Britain and North America, designers and architects, especially those involved in the Arts & Crafts movement such as William Morris and Charles Voysey, all used and/or designed decorative tiles for floors and walls. But the most renowned tile designer of the era was a potter, William de Morgan, who started designing tiles for Morris & Co. in about 1869. De Morgan studied Persian and Turkish patterns and colors, and his tiles had characteristic flowing floral and animal motifs. Many Victorian families gathered around the statutory focal point of the home – a hearth – which was decorated with beautiful de Morgan tile panels.

Boldly decorated wall tiles and encaustic floor tiles were also being used for bathrooms, which were starting to be installed in grander houses; restrooms in gentlemen's clubs; the "health clubs" of the period – Turkish baths; and conservatories, smoking rooms and hallways in domestic, commercial and public buildings. Tiled panels were used to decorate retailers' walls where hygiene was important – dairies, butchers' shops, grocers, restaurants and bars – and they added a little cheer to institutions such as museums and city halls, libraries and other civic buildings. Once again, churches were decorated with encaustic tiles as part of the then-popular Gothic revival, as was the Palace of Westminster in London.

In the 1920's and 30's, tiles were still used in homes for fireplaces, kitchens and also by the rapidly expanding bathroom industry, where Art Deco styling was popular. However, designs and colors tended to be "safer" and less exciting than in earlier decades and rarely provided the central theme in a room. Tiles were used to much more dramatic effect in architecture – on the walls of rail stations; for the façades of stores, hotels and restaurants; to clad the exterior of modern buildings in order to provide color and contrast to the new building materials of concrete and glass.

Today, there is a vast array of tiles available in myriad colors and patterns. In addition to the wealth of traditional tile designs which survive from centuries past, there are a multitude of modern tiles in exciting colors and shapes. All these tiles can be used creatively for floors, walls, around fireplaces, behind sinks and on countertops, as dados and dado rails. And when it comes to the way they can be arranged, it is like looking through a kaleidoscope – the permutations are endless.

You will find lots of ideas within the pages of this book which will help you create a specific style or look. You will quickly discover that designing with tiles is made easier by the fact they are usually produced to a geometric module – square, rectangular, hexagonal, octagonal, etc. Plain, attractively colored tiles can be used simply to create a patchwork, striped or checkerboard effect. There are also infinite possibilities with patterned tiles, or with a mixture of plain or slightly textured field tiles, teamed with borders and drop-ins. They can also be used to form a border, panel or mural.

Remember that tiles do not have to be confined conventionally to the bathroom and kitchen – they are a practical alternative to wood flooring, especially in areas of heavy wear like halls. A tiled dado in a hall, porch or dining room will be an interesting and practical design feature. Or a conservatory wall can be tiled in combination with a fountain or other water feature. Tiles can form an important part of furniture design, such as a tiled table top ... anywhere where a practical, wipable, heatproof surface is required. They can also be used to refurbish old furniture – to give a new lease of life to a Victorian washstand, for example.

Wherever your personal tastes lie, and whatever your level of experience, this book will give you plenty of ideas and all the information you need to achieve the look you require, be it a sundrenched Mediterranean conservatory or a hi-tech kitchen – the possibilities are endless.

▶ This kaleidoscope of tiles shows the infinite palette of colors available and how they can be used to create stunning effects, illusions and patterns. [Langley]

A HISTORY OF TILE STYLES

Mosaics can be made from clay, glass, marble, etc. Most people associate mosaics with the Romans who created stunning floors. Modern mosaics are often still arranged in traditional Roman designs.

Roman-style mosaics

The flourishing trade with the **Orient** in the 17th and 18th centuries led to the westward spread of Eastern designs and manufacturing techniques. The use of Oriental motifs and forms in Western interior decoration became increasingly popular in the 18th century, and they are still widely used today.

Influences from the Orient

Traditional Gothic patterns

The Victorians, led by Pugin, loved **Gothic** designs. They were mock-medieval, heavy designs executed in rich, deep colors with intricate patterns and motifs.

Islamic tiles have also been made since ancient times and continue to influence modern tile designers. They are best known for their rich colors and intricate flowing designs.

European nations, such as Holland, took the new techniques and designs from around the world and developed their own distinctive tiles. **Dutch Delftware** is named after the town of Delft, famous for tin-glazed earthenware. The designs, in characteristic blue and white, copied the Oriental porcelain brought to Europe by the Dutch East India Company. The traditional blue and white figurative and simple geometric patterns are still copied today.

Islamic designs

Dutch Delftware

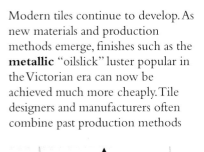

Modern tiles continue to develop. As new materials and production methods emerge, finishes such as the **metallic** "oilslick" luster popular in the Victorian era can now be achieved much more cheaply. Tile designers and manufacturers often combine past production methods

Oilslick metallics

with modern designs and vice versa. The secret medieval method of producing inlaid tiles – **encaustics** – was rediscovered in the 19th century when it enjoyed a 70-year revival. Today, it is once again becoming popular and is used to produce both traditional and modern tile designs.

The **Arts & Crafts** movement, spearheaded by William Morris in the mid/late 19th century, was a reaction to heavy Victorian style and was dedicated to bringing back

Arts & Crafts design by William de Morgan

simple design and high standards of craftsmanship. The British artist-potter William de Morgan was a friend of Morris and became one of the most important designers in the development of ceramic tile design in the 19th century. His tiles were often used in the grand bathrooms which were being installed by the nobility and emerging middle classes, as well as in entrance halls and around fireplaces.

Art Nouveau was a decorative style popular at the turn of the century, with emphasis on sinuous flowing lines. It developed partially from the Arts & Crafts movement.

The **Art Deco** style of design became fashionable between 1910 and 1930 and was characterized by solid rectilinear shapes, and geometric and stylized motifs, some with an Egyptian flavor. In its purest form, it relied on expressive exotic features.

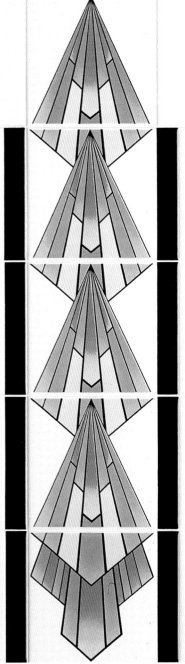

Art Nouveau   Art Deco

Encaustic tiles with modern designs

However, modern tile designers do not draw purely on the past for their inspiration. New, innovative styles, such as the wide choice of exciting **abstract** designs, continue to develop and will do so as long as the beauty of tiles exerts its magical power.

Modern abstracts

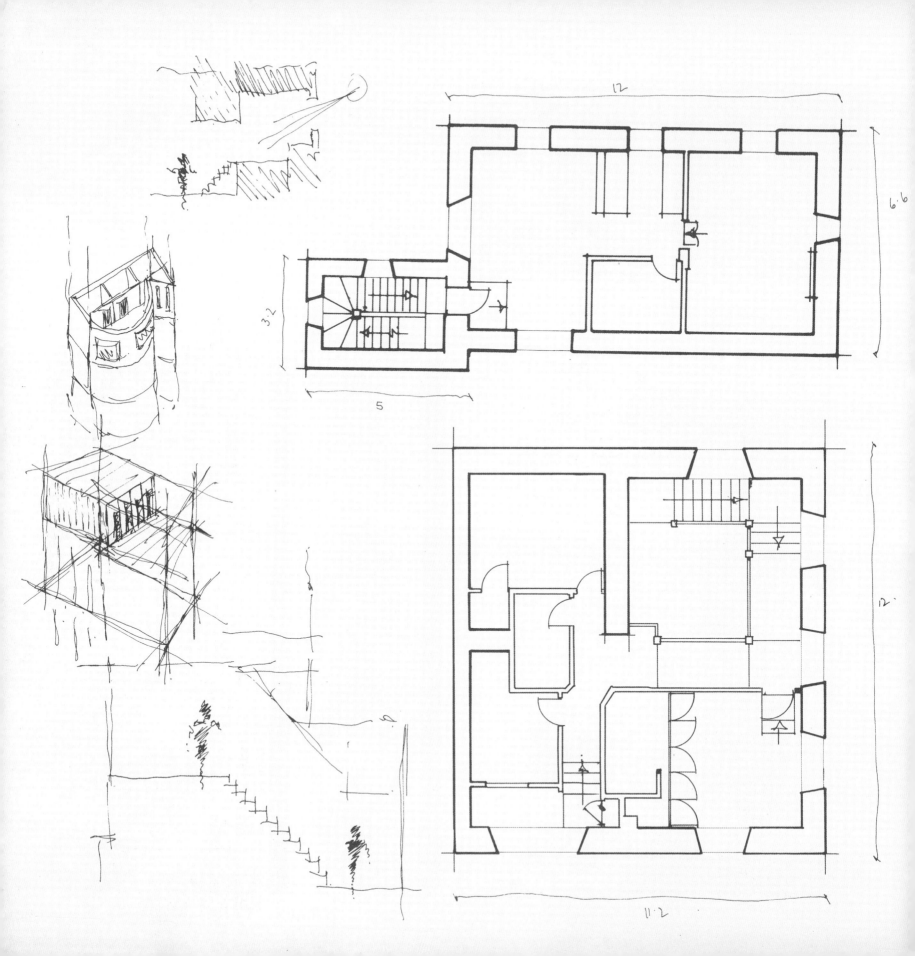

ROOM
DIRECTORY

HALLS

Y ou get only one chance to make a first impression, so the entrance hall — the area of the home seen initially by visitors — should be warm, welcoming and make a definite statement. At the same time it can be planned to hint at the style and colors used in the surrounding rooms. Such constructive visual links also help to make a small house or apartment seem much more spacious, especially if a similar color is used for the flooring throughout. The hall is a transitional area, so you can be brave and bold with color and pattern.

You can also use some visual decorating "tricks" to make a small hall look larger or one of baronial proportions seem more cozy and intimate, and to adjust the proportions so ceilings do not seem so tall, or make a long, narrow hall look less like a tunnel.

An entrance hall often takes a great deal of punishment – from dirty shoes and sticky fingers; buggy and bicycle wheels; luggage; shopping and all the things which have to be brought into or taken out of the house. So the hall is a hard-working area which needs a practical treatment for all the major surfaces – the floor, walls (especially at the side of the staircase) and woodwork.

Floors

A good interior designer begins with the floor. If you have an existing hard (permanent) flooring, consider refurbishment and repair, rather than replacement – or if this is unavoidable, call in a salvage expert to take up the old flooring as your "white elephant" might be someone else's dream product!

Choose a new hall floor treatment that is washable and hard-wearing; also consider safety – floors should always be non-trip and non-slip. In an older property, you might opt for brick, slate, terracotta *carrés,* flagstones or even reconstituted "pavers," which may come in some lovely soft ice-cream colors as well as traditional "stone." In an elegant Regency or neoclassical interior, a traditional black-and-white checkerboard floor or diamond design with black insets, possibly edged with a Greek-key border, can be created in ceramic tiles, or in marble for an extra opulent touch.

Victorian or Edwardian floors might be tiled in authentic creamy beige, terracotta, black and vivid

◀ A bold red and green tiled dado with raised beading and a decorative frieze suggests a return to turn-of-the-century elegance. It is offset by a black and white diamond checkerboard floor with a dramatic border which emphasizes the unusual shape. [H&R Johnson]

▼ Earthenware *carrés* used to floor an entrance area are continued onto the stair treads in a typical French-style interior. Each area in the open-plan space is defined with contrasting border tiles. [Société Carré]

◀ The natural textures of rustic wood and simple plastered walls create a warm welcome in a country cottage-style hall. The contrast with the silver-blue slate floor, which has a natural vitality, gives an impression of space. [Fired Earth]

▲ The subtle contrasts in tone of the richly colored Spanish terracotta handmade floor tiles create a warm Mediterranean look, which is enhanced by a contrasting turquoise and yellow border. [Paris Ceramics]

◀ Terracotta tiles laid trellis fashion are bordered in black and white to define the shape of the floor. [Country Floors]

▶ Mexican natural-clay floor tiles are combined with an inset geometric pattern to provide added visual interest. [Corres Mexican Tiles]

◀ Cool blue wall tiles in a trellis pattern provide an infill above a deeper colored dado. Contrasting dado beading and borders add elegance and enhance the coordinating *trompe l'oeil* treatment. [Country Floors]

▼ An 8-tile-wide panel using different tile types shows how wall tiles can be combined to create maximum visual effect. [Decorum Ceramic Studio]

blue patterned encaustic tiles. Alternatively, interesting patterns can be created with black, terracotta and beige quarry tiles for less expense, perhaps with an encaustic tile border or "drop in" feature tile. All these treatments need to be suitably dressed to make them easy to care for and long lasting.

If there is a stair carpet, the visual link will be strengthened if it echoes the color and pattern of the hall floor. Where room floors meet the hall floor in doorways, use individual wooden thresholds to seal the join and paint or stain them to match the main color. This will look coordinated, much more elegant and less obtrusive than a metal strip.

Walls

Halls, which take a lot of punishment, need to be washable – they can be wood clad, painted (perhaps using a specialist technique), or hung with vinyl wallcovering, etc. If the walls are tall, a split-level treatment can be very effective and helps to reduce the height visually. A defining plaster or wooden dado rail placed horizontally about a yard (1m) up from the floor allows for different decorating techniques to be used. For instance, apply and paint a textured surface on the area below the rail and paper the area above it with a suitable pattern.

For a really practical and unusual decorative treatment, apply ceramic tiles to the lower wall, finishing with a tiled border, nosing or dado rail. The tiles can be patterned, or plain tiles could be arranged to create a patchwork or trellis effect. In a large hall, a specially commissioned *trompe l'oeil* effect could decorate the lower part of the wall.

Color

Look towards the warmer, welcoming end of the spectrum – rich reds, soft peach, earthy terracottas, sunny yellows, glowing golds, apricots, burnished chestnuts, exciting pinks, pumpkin orange . . . If you use a cool color or a neutral on the floor, introduce warmer shades in the wall treatments.

◀ A hall leading to a patio is floored with rich terracotta and buff tiles laid in a diamond pattern to enlarge the width of the floor area visually. [The Merchant Tiler]

▼◀ Large flagstones are laid in the hall and throughout the ground floor to create visual unity in a traditional setting. [Ann Sacks]

▼ A natural stone floor sets a classic, timeless theme and emphasizes the use of natural textures, such as plastic walls and wood. [Ann Sacks]

LIVING ROOMS

In many homes, the living room is a multi-functional area, used by all the family for eating, entertaining, watching television, playing games or with toys, listening to (and performing) music; in other households, one room may be set aside as a family room, and the living room is used only on more formal occasions. In the former situation, the materials and furniture need to be versatile and the color scheme practical, and all the surfaces should be robust and easy to clean. In a less-used room, the scheme can be more elegant, the colors more delicate, and the surfaces more fragile.

In both types of living room – functional and formal – the seating must be comfortable, the storage facilities practical, and the lighting should relate to the various uses to which the room is put. Never lose sight of the basic concept of good design, i.e. achieving a perfect combination of the practical and the aesthetic.

As one of the rooms in the home used for rest and relaxation, choose colors, patterns and textures which are as easy on the eye as they are to care for. Use middle tones for the main surfaces (the floor, walls and upholstery fabrics), restrained patterns and interesting textures. Stimulating color accents and unusual shapes can be added in small quantities, or as accessories, to provide an extra visual dimension.

The floor gets a great deal of wear and tear in this much-used room, so aim to design from the floor up, if possible. It makes sense to choose a flooring which is hard-wearing, easy to clean, and does not show every spill and mark. Use the floor to sample and color-match when working on the rest of the scheme.

If the living room is integrated with the kitchen or dining area, or has a conservatory, veranda or sun

◀ The terracotta flooring is taken through from the living room into the hallway to create a visual link and make the whole area look more spacious. [Ann Sacks]

◀◀ Warm-colored terracotta and bleached blonde flagstones are laid in a country-style living room and sealed to create a glowing patina. [Ann Sacks]

▼ Handmade "old terracotta" tiles are individually distressed to give the impression of a well-worn floor and create a traditional, warm ambience in the working area of an elegant living room. [Fired Earth]

room leading from it, coordinate the various schemes and consider using the same hard flooring throughout (flagstones, quarry or slate tiles, earthenware *carrés*, brick, matte ceramic tiles, etc.). This can be softened with rugs, coir, seagrass or rush matting to help define the sitting area. Always consider safety, and make sure floor coverings do not slip or trip people, and that furniture will not slide across the floor.

Selecting a Style

First of all, consider the basic architectural character of the room in relation to the way you use the space. The size, shape, orientation and amount of natural daylight which the room receives are constraints which could dictate a suitable style – be it modern or with a specific period flavor. You may have a cherished existing item – such as a piece of furniture, fabrics, a rug or other accessory – around which you want to design the scheme. If the room is a basic bland "box," you can impose almost any style on it, as long as it is not too enclosing.

Choose the color scheme in relation to the style as well as in consideration of the ambience you want to create. In a room for relaxation, choose pale, cool tones, work to a monochromatic theme, or use the natural/neutral range. For a more intimate, cozy atmosphere, look towards the richer, warmer colors – subtle reds, earthy terracottas, elegant rose, deep golds. If the room is small, work with the paler values of the warm colors – soft pinks, apricots and peach, pale yellows, buttercreams. Always remember the golden good decorating rule: add some cool color contrast to emphasize the warm effect.

Focal Points

This room, more than any other in the home, needs a focal point. Traditionally, this feature was a

◄◄ Mosaics are used as a border in a library/living room in order to divide the reading and writing areas and to suggest a rug. The flooring is carried up onto the plinth of the shelves to make the area seem wider. [Country Floors]

▲▶ The true "heart of the home" is the living room fireplace – as true now as it was in past centuries, despite central heating! Here, different tiled panels create colorful and decorative insets between the cast-iron grate and the more imposing facing. When selecting a living room fireplace, make sure the scale is right – an overpowering construction can spoil the balance of the room. [Chiswick Fireplaces] fireplace or stove, which is comfortable and warm to group seating around for talking, watching television, playing games or listening to music. In the summer it may be more practical to reposition the furniture so the outside becomes the focal point – choose window treatments to dramatize and enhance the view of the garden.

A fireplace, chimneypiece or stove could be the starting point for the scheme, as well as the focal point. If you install a new one, make sure it is the correct scale in relation to the size of the room (from the heat output aspect as well as the visual aspect).

From the practical point of view, brick, stone, ceramic tiles and slate are all heat-resistant, and are a wise choice for hearths, wall areas and chimney breasts backing free-standing stoves or as an integral part of the fireplace.

Marble or carved wooden fire surrounds look classically elegant, and come in a wide range of shapes and styles, from Jacobean and neoclassical to traditional "swagged" designs. Stone or brick-clad chimney breasts or inglenooks will be suitably rustic in a country house or cottage setting. A continental or Scandinavian-style stove can be fully tiled and set on a tiled hearth against a tiled wall area. Cast-iron or enameled wood-burning stoves can be similarly treated and positioned on a heat-proof hearth.

In a Victorian or Edwardian setting, choose a black cast-iron grate with decorated tiled inset and hearth, and wooden overmantel. For a specific Arts & Crafts theme, try to find suitable tile designs by William de Morgan, William Morris or Walter Crane; for an Art Nouveau theme, there are tiles available in the Charles Rennie Mackintosh image. For a 1920s/30s Art Deco setting, you will need to search for a typical fully tiled fireplace surround and hearth; alternatively, you can design one using suitable geometric tiles sympathetic to the period.

◄ Bold blue and white handpainted octagonal tiles, combined with plain blue triangles and a neat Izmir border in the 17th-century Majolica tradition, form a practical and eye-catching focal point behind the cast-iron wood-burning stove in this country-style living room. [Fired Earth]

◄ The fireplace and fireback, in Dutch Delft-tile tradition, have authentic motifs painted on the glazed tiles. Such tiles must be fireproof if they are used in an open fire. They can be combined with stoves or used as a decorative focal point and filled with plants and flowers during summer. [Country Floors]

◄ The blue-and-white diamond tiles of the fireplace and hearth look like a handcrafted Shaker-style patchwork. [Country Floors]

▼ Subtle gray-green tiles on the hearth and mantelpiece frame the fireplace and are combined with warm terracotta on the floor. [Ann Sacks]

KITCHENS AND DINING ROOMS

The kitchen is often seen rather romantically as the "heart of the home." This mood is reinforced with the current nostalgic trend towards the rustic, real wood, country-style kitchen — complete with old-fashioned range, ceramic sink, potted herbs, dried flowers and basketware. But it is also the main work area or nerve center of the home. Nowadays a dining room may be part of the kitchen, or also used as a workroom or playroom. Such multipurpose areas need careful planning, furnishing and decorating.

The Kitchen

A kitchen consequently needs hard-wearing materials on floors, walls, units and countertops to provide impervious, hygienic and easy-to-clean surfaces. Ceramic tiles are a practical and decorative solution. They can be used as "splashbacks" behind cooking areas, sink and food preparation areas, and as work surfaces on units and tables. Riven slate, stone, quarry and ceramic tiles, and earthenware *carrés* are all possible floorings, which can be sealed to make them easy to care for and long lasting, and treated to be non-slip. With a clever choice of color and texture, these treatments will not look stark or feel harsh and unyielding underfoot.

Kitchens can often be cold, clinical places, despite the hot and steamy activities which take place in them. A radiator is sometimes not installed because of the presence of an oven; however, with good insulation the appliances give off very little heat. To counterbalance the cold, look towards warmer, more inviting colors for the main surfaces – the floor, walls, ceiling, cabinets and woodwork, and window treatments; the harsh look of wall tiles can be softened with some light-filtering textures – for instance, cane, trellis, shutters, slatted blinds or sheer fabric café curtains; a rug or natural floorcovering can be used to define the floor in dining/sitting areas; place terracotta pots planted with herbs or brightly colored flowers on available surfaces.

A warm kitchen can be cooled with a soft green, minty tone, faded Shaker blue, or a romantic lilac color scheme. Shiny, reflective textures also have a cooling effect and help to increase the apparent size of a small kitchen.

Stylish Selection

A kitchen should be as carefully themed as any other room in the home, to give it an overall mood and

▲ The texture of warm rose Venetian marble tiles on this splashback sets off a decorative *Herbes de Provence* inset tiled border. [Fired Earth]

▲▶ A counter of stoneware tiles is combined with a colorful French Fauve-style border, set into a white glazed splashback. [Fired Earth]

◀ A patchwork effect is obtained with hand-glazed, dragged tiles in exotic colors, hung trellis fashion and grouted in white. [Decorum Ceramic Studio/Miscellanea of Churt]

▶ Highly glazed vivid blue tiles matching the range form a decorative heat-proof backing inside the recess, and are bordered in unglazed terracotta tiles for extra visual impact. [Fired Earth]

ambience. Choose the floor and wall tiles to enhance the basic style of your kitchen – rustic pavers, brick, warm terracottas, heathery quarries and continental earthenware slabs will all complement a country-style kitchen with pine, distressed or painted furniture. Display copper utensils and touches of brass to add to the warm, welcoming feel.

Add an appropriate flavor to a period scheme using specific patterns such as traditional blue and white Delft; richly colored Arts and Crafts patterned wall and border tiles; sunny, exotic Mediterranean glazes; or flora, vegetable and fauna designs. Alternatively, combine sleek, glossy, geometric patterns on wall tiles with slate, marble, granite or terrazzo flooring (non-slip) for a more modern, minimalist scheme.

Plain wall and floor tiles can be used to great effect. Use two tones (light and dark), or strongly contrasting colors – such as turquoise blue and terracotta, red and green, yellow and lilac, black and white, brown and cream – to create a checkerboard or striped effect. This treatment can visually enlarge a small floor, especially if it relates to the color of the cupboards, or if the baseboard (skirting) is decorated to match the floor. Or use a contrasting color, or specific pattern, to create a border effect to help define separate areas – for instance, to divide the kitchen from the dining area, or the utility room from the kitchen, or to outline an important feature such as a recess, window frame or hutch (dresser).

On a large wall area, tiles can be cut and hung in a more unusual way – for example, set diamond-fashion on a dado. Panels could be created on a big, blank area for different effects – for instance, a mural could be painted in the center panel; or tiles could be arranged to suggest a "room-with-a-view" where there is no window; or a softly graduated

▲ This kitchen in classic blue and white has wooden counters and a related tile splashback. [World's End Tiles]

◄◄ Tiles of fish and fruit are combined with decorative border tiles to form a practical counter for food preparation and visual interest in a windowless area. [Country Floors]

▲ Heavy relief decoration on glazed tiles in white and soft neutrals adds textural interest to an area. Neutral colored tiles give flexibility to the overall color scheme. [Ann Sacks]

◄ Plain terracotta and navy-blue tiles are hung to create a subtle horizontal striped effect, enhancing a country kitchen style. [H&R Johnson]

monochromatic effect could be created using tiles in different tones of one color (start with the paler values of the color at ceiling height and work down to the deeper tones at floor level).

A plain or dull tiled wall can be enlivened by using a different or unusual colored grouting, instead of the conventional white or beige, or "background to the tile" color – for instance, strong yellow with plain white tiles; deep green with pale pink or beige; royal blue with apricot or peach; terracotta or deep Indian red with pale green or soft yellow. However, charcoal gray or black tiles can look stunning grouted in white. Some colored groutings are available ready-mixed, or you can mix your own.

The Dining Room

The style, pattern and color scheme for a dining room depends to some extent – like the kitchen – on the meals you serve, and the type of cooking and entertaining you do. As with all successful decorating, consideration needs to be given to the size, shape, orientation and the architectural character of the room but aim to create a cozy, intimate ambience.

Nowadays a dining room may be a part of the living room or kitchen, or it may have to double as a study, workroom or playroom. Such multipurpose areas need very careful planning, furnishing and decorating if they are to be functional as well as elegant. The dining area should echo the style, color scheme and theme of the rest of the room.

If you have a separate dining room which is mainly used for more formal entertaining and important family gatherings, aim to make it really special. Give it a distinctive style or period flavor which is warm and inviting, to encourage family and guests to enjoy and linger over a lovingly prepared meal.

◄◄ African slate flooring in warm buff, burnt orange and gray contrast with the shiny black granite countertops and the range, which in turn acts as a foil for the wooden cabinets. [Naturestone Design Village]

Chairs should be comfortable, with practical (washable) covers, and of the correct height to relate well to an ample table (i.e. plenty of space for diners' knees and elbows). There should be adequate storage for glasses, china, flatware (cutlery), linen and other dining table items, and heat-proof food-serving facilities.

Choose appetite-inducing colors from the warmer side of the spectrum, such as deep wine or burgundy reds, rich rose, sugar pinks, earthy terracottas, glowing yellows and golds teamed with gleaming mahogany or waxed pine; or more subtle ice-cream colors, such as strawberry, raspberry, peach, apricot, lime or citron teamed with cream and a little pistachio or herb green.

Brighten up a dark dining room with sharp lemon, warm gold or sunflower yellow, spiked with white and contrasted with sky blue or grass green to suggest sunshine and the

▲ An all-tiled kitchen – floor, walls, countertops, cabinet recess – creates a subtle country effect in a small apartment kitchen. The floor pattern expands the space visually. [Country Floors]

◄ An elegant kitchen, with a riven slate floor in coordinating shades of gray and blue, provides a cool ambience for cooking, washing and other steamy activities. [Stonell]

▶ This scheme relies on rustic textures, sharpened with copper and opalescent glass, to provide visual contrast. The subtle color of the tiled area around the stove makes the scheme less obtrusive. [Ann Sacks]

warmth of long summer days. In a large space, red and green, or a gold and red scheme, can help to set a Scottish theme, especially if tartan plaid or checks and suitable accessories are selected.

Stylish Schemes

Dining room styling can be modern, simple and streamlined. The warm, rich, earthy color and rustic textures associated with the currently popular Mediterranean look will suggest meals eaten *al fresco* in Provence, Tuscany or on a Greek island. To emulate, combine a deep blue ceiling with a terracotta-tiled floor and introduce some ocher yellow to contrast – for an outdoor look, stenciled vine leaves or bunches of grapes could echo the pattern on a tiled table top or wall area.

For a sleek Scandinavian or minimalist modern style, use teak or light wood furniture, creamy neutral colors and natural textures combined with colorful accents in china and glassware. Soften the floors with shaggy non-slip rugs. For a more metropolitan mood, combine black ash furniture with a gray granite table top, black and white

checkerboard tiled floor, and again some colorful accessories to lighten the scheme.

For a traditional look, opt for a specific period flavor. A Georgian, colonial or Regency theme is very popular for dining rooms, partly because there is so much good dining furniture available in yew, mahogany, and light and dark oak. These woods look good teamed with rich textures and enhanced with warm reds and golds and touches of brass, and with Oriental rugs or rush mats on flagstone floors.

To create a country cottage ambience, a golden pine scrubbed table and waxed sideboard combined with distressed or painted furniture in slightly faded "Shaker colors" (i.e. soft denim blues and gray-greens) can be set on a burnt orange quarry-tiled or earthenware slabbed floor.

For an Arts & Crafts look, team a limed or light oak refectory table with a matching sideboard, tall-backed rush-seated chairs and authentic William Morris wallcoverings and/or fabrics. A traditional fireplace could be the starting point for such a scheme, with cast-iron grate and tiled inset.

A Practical Approach

Surfaces in a dining room must be easy to clean as occasional spillages are unavoidable. Walls may be splashed when bottles are opened and food served. To be really practical, surfaces need to be heat-proof – a ceramic-tiled top can be a boon on a unit, sideboard or serving table. A matching tiled "splashback" for the wall behind the serving area is a feature worth considering. If it fits the style of the room, a capacious Victorian or Edwardian washstand with tiled or marble top and back can be a practical alternative.

The floor should be equally practical, and preferably washable. The suggestions outlined for kitchens are all applicable for a dining room.

▶ A 17th-century-style dining room in a country house with rich, dark wood furniture is enhanced by reclaimed traditional French terracotta floor tiles and warm pink color-washed walls. [Fired Earth]

▲ A terracotta tiled floor is used for a conservatory dining area. The border detail defines the space, and the floor provides good color contrast with white walls/furniture. [Oak Leaf Conservatories]

CONSERVATORIES

Some houses have a conservatory, sun room, porch, gazebo or veranda as part of the architecture. Those built in the eighteenth or nineteenth century (or at the turn of the century) may already have a fabulous floor – highly decorative encaustic tiles or flagstones were often laid in such areas; quarry tiles in terracotta, beige and black; brick pavers; or even traditional black and white marble in the grander properties. If it is necessary to do a little refurbishment of such an existing floor, call in an expert to help restore it to its former glory.

However, if this type of floor is not to your taste, a salvage expert can remove it and sell it to somebody else, giving you some extra budget to put towards a new floor.

When considering flooring for conservatories, porches, verandas, etc., bear in mind that it needs to be impervious to damp and easy to clean – there will be drips from plant watering and mud tramped in from outside. The surface could be continued onto the patio, or down the front walk (path) to the gate – a fashion in former times – to create continuity and a visual link.

It is wise to choose a frost-proof quality tile, slate or stone, since the floor can become very cold in winter, especially if it has absorbed water – a strong shaft of sunlight, magnified by a glazed roof or large window, shining onto a very cold floor can cause it to crack. If the surface is porous, it needs to be adequately sealed to protect it from the elements.

Master Planning

Most conservatories, porches, verandas, etc., are an extension to the main house, built to provide extra living space and other facilities; porches and some verandas are incorporated to enhance the entrance and cut out drafts. If you wish to add an extra room, plan the use of space carefully, working out exactly what function you wish the area to perform, and then furnish and equip it accordingly.

If a conservatory or sun room is to contain exotic plants, and be partially used as a greenhouse, it will need carefully controlled ventilation, sun screening, and possibly automatic watering facilities. Glazing should always be double, and in some cases triple, and in vulnerable situations – such as when the extension is used as a playroom – use special shatter-proof laminated glass to avoid accidents.

However much glass is used in the construction of such an extension,

▲ A small conservatory dining room is floored with antique yellow terracotta tiles laid with dark slate keystones to create an illusion of greater width. [Paris Ceramics]

◀ Traditional "Torquemada" terracotta tiles have been personalized with a stenciled decorative pattern and fleur-de-lys motif. [Paris Ceramics]

▶ Octagonal Mexican terracotta tiles with square inset provide warmth and textural interest all year round. The upholstery echoes the color and shape of the floor tiles. [Corres Mexican tiles]

light will always be lost from the adjoining area. To counteract this, decorate both the extension and the adjoining spaces in pale or sunny colors and include some light-reflecting surfaces. As for any room, a coordinating theme used throughout creates an impression of unity and spaciousness, especially if the floor is the same or a similar color.

Conservatories, verandas and sun rooms can be styled and furnished as carefully as any other room. A "return to the Raj" look can be created by using neutral colors and natural textures, with cane or wicker furniture, ceiling fans, slatted wooden or rattan blinds under sheer drapes, and terracotta floor tiles or brick pavers, all enhanced by suitable

plants and colorful containers to provide accents.

For an extension intended mainly for family living or dining, consider a Regency theme – delicate white wrought-iron furniture and stone floors offset with rich reds and golds; or a neoclassical style, with black and white tiled floor, elegant pillars, Wedgwood blue walls and ceiling,

and touches of terracotta and black. A successful Gothic look requires suitable fenestration – tall, slim windows with pointed tops – and introduce a glass-topped table on black iron trestles with matching black iron chairs and accessories, including curtain poles and candle and light fixtures. The color scheme can be mainly a gray monochromatic

◀ This exotic Moorish-style indoor atrium is decorated in discreet neutrals. The antique *blanc rose* terracotta floor with antique barr cabochons acts as a foil to the richly colored furniture. [Paris Ceramics]

▲ A classic clay fountain (the faucet makes plant watering easier) framed with decorative glazed Moroccan tiles is set against a background of white mosaics. [Country Floors]

◀ A fully glazed conservatory can be used to raise plants and bonsai trees, as well as for summer dining. The pale terracotta blinds echo the color of the earthenware floor tiles. [Malbrook Conservatories]

▼ This Gothic-style conservatory has a stone floor with inset diamond border design to emphasize the shape of the room. [Stonell]

one, accented with scarlet, purple and mauve. Or for a more modern, minimalist setting, choose stream-lined Italianate furniture in chrome and glass, enhanced by a neutral color scheme and primary accents.

When the space is to be specifically used for dining, you might prefer an *al fresco* Mediterranean theme. Aim to echo the look of open-air sun-baked patios and tile the floor with earthenware *carrés* in rich burnt orange; paint walls with an ocher glaze over white-painted brick; and bring in a strong bright or sky blue to contrast. Introduce some pictorial ceramic wall tile panels to create an impression of a view, and accessorize with suitable plants and vines – these could be trained to form a sun canopy overhead.

Pictorial tiled wall treatments also come into their own in pool houses and games rooms – these could be specially commissioned to follow a specific theme. Traditional patterned terrazzo flooring, stone or brick are all warm and safe to walk on (floors surrounding pools must be non-slip), and sunshine colors of yellows, golds, terracottas, peach, buttermilk and black, combined with some brilliant blue, will add warmth and elegance.

Utility Rooms
Utility rooms usually lead off the kitchen, porch or conservatory, and are the area of the home which takes the most "punishment" of all. Its

practical uses are endless, varying from repotting plants or growing seedlings, to scouring pots and pans. This area may also contain the freezer, cupboards and racks for long-term vegetable and dry goods storage, a washing machine, dryer and ironing equipment, etc. It may also double as a hobby area and be the only place in the house to store tools.

The floor should ideally be easy to scrub and mop, and be impervious to spillages, breakages, and muddy paw and foot marks. Choose a permanent "hard" surface in a practical middle-tone color. Many of the floorings suggested for kitchens are equally suitable for a utility room – for example, riven slate, flagstones, non-slip ceramic tiles, quarried or reconstituted stone slabs, brick (sealed), earthenware *carrés* and quarry tiles.

Apart from cupboards, shelves and racks, etc., there should be adequate drainers and work surfaces – especially to either side of any (deep) sink – and a generous-sized table. If space is short, consider a butcher's block on wheels or a folding or drop-down-flap table – or one which pulls/folds out from a storage unit. Again, the surface should be easy to clean, and scrub if necessary, so some of the suggested floorings can be used as countertops and splashbacks, creating a feeling of continuity. Make sure any grouting is hygienic and impervious to cooking liquids, acids, etc.

Choose colors to contribute to the visual link between the utility room and the room from which it leads. Warmer tones will soften and take the chill off a rather clinical and utilitarian area, which may be filled with fairly harsh textures and shiny surfaces. Patterns and colors can also be bolder in this room – it is a good place for a stimulating scheme – perhaps using complementary (contrasting) colors, or a neutral color with some very bright accents.

◀ A simple glazed extension creates a sunny summer living room. The classic white tiled floor with black key square insets is enhanced by the colorful rattan furniture; white vertical blinds form an adjustable sunscreen. [Wickes]

◀ An all-white conservatory is floored with soft blue-gray slate slabs laid at an angle to expand the area visually. [Malbrook Conservatories]

▲ An elegant Palladian-style garden room is floored with classic limestone flag-stones and faded blue insets. [Paris Ceramics]

▶ Encaustic and geometric floor tiles recreate the original 1860 tiled conservatory floor at the prestigious Hurlingham Club in London, England. [H&R Johnson]

BATHROOMS AND BEDROOMS

The bathroom, downstairs "powder room" and shower room are utilitarian areas of the home which are often cold and clinical and rather uncomfortable, and generally not as carefully styled as other rooms in the home. But as modern plumbing becomes more efficient and we develop sybaritic tendencies, the bathroom is being filled with more complex equipment and is now a room in which to enjoy oneself. It may also be converted to a dual purpose fitness and personal hygiene room. Bedrooms are usually highly personal spaces and can be decorated and furnished in a more individual way than other rooms.

The Bathroom

Unless you are doing major building, refurbishment or conversion work, the bathroom is usually the smallest room in the house and needs careful planning in order to fit everything in, and clever color scheming and decorative treatments to make it appear more spacious. Mirrors and mirror tiles help to magnify space and reflect both natural day and night time artificial light. Mirrors and mirror tiles must be hung on a perfectly flat surface to avoid distorted reflections – rough walls can be clad with special wall or plaster board first, or the tiles can be mounted onto chipboard or hardboard panels.

Comfortable Colors

Bathrooms tend to be cold because there are so many clinical surfaces and shiny textures. The bath, basin, shower tray/stall, toilet, etc., are all designed to withstand dirt and damp, and the form of these items is often harsh and unyielding. Gleaming chrome taps and rails, glossy white ceramic tiles (or shiny cold marble), enameled cast-iron baths, and glass shower screens all add to this unwelcoming impression. Soft textures will offset these light-reflecting ones – for instance, fluffy bath towels and mats, possibly trimmed with embroidery or crochet; lace, gauze or other sheer fabric for curtains or blinds; baskets filled with soaps and other toiletries; plants chosen for their steam-loving properties and for variation in shape and texture.

In a small, dark windowless bathroom consider creating a *trompe l'oeil* effect with a tiled panel suggesting a view or seascape; or use a mirror or mirror tiles to simulate a window and "dress" it with curtains or blinds subtly lit with concealed pelmet lighting.

Choose paler tones of colors, or a monochromatic (one-color) effect to

enlarge a small space visually. Use stronger colors in a bigger room, or some bold contrasts for a more stimulating atmosphere (in a busy bathroom, where you want to encourage fast throughput!) – for maximum effect, mix complementary (contrasting) colors.

To create a warm and welcoming bathroom, the sunshine colors – pale yellow, apricot, dusty brick, soft coral and faded gold – teamed with warm whites, and accented with some brilliant sky blue, will create a summery feel all the year round. Alternatively, combine coffee with creams and terracotta, sharpened with strong jade green; or look to a floral theme for inspiration, such as the crisp pinks, soft mauves, golden yellows and creams found in a bunch of freesias, cooled down with soft spring green.

Careful Coordination

The starting point will probably have to be the existing color and style of the sanitaryware (bath, basin, toilet, etc.) which is already installed. Accurate color-matching is essential; you must look at proposed materials in the bathroom under exact lighting conditions. The sanitaryware may be a cold color – for example, "pampas" or "whisper" grays and greens, or even blue; other popular colors in the past include burgundy red, tan-orange, very dark blue, and even black. These are all very difficult bathroom colors as, contrary to

▷ A stunning custom-designed shower room: the *trompe l'oeil* effect is created using glass mosaics. [Mosaic Workshops]

◁◁ A recessed sink in a large bathroom is adorned with flowers. The vanity unit is tiled in coordination with the wall tiles and also with the pattern on the basin. [Country Floors]

◁ A mirrored alcove forms a decorative focal point in a bedroom. Patterned and plain tiles create a "frame" for the mirror and provide an attractive display shelf for personal items. [Société Carré]

popular belief, they show up every mark as an unappealing gray scum.

A strong-colored set cannot be toned down or hidden by combining it with safe neutrals. The only way to detract from an anti-social, bright color is to use a very bold treatment which "shouts back at it," or to create a monochromatic scheme using the suite color as the darkest tone. Pick a wallcovering or tiles which incorporate the main color but also introduce some strong contrasts. Echo these colors in your window treatments, flooring and accessories.

If you are lucky enough to be starting a bathroom from scratch, choose sanitaryware which allows for flexible styling and has future design and color scheming possibilities. White is a classic choice and has endless possible schematic permutations, although it can be cold; some of the ivory, champagne and soft "blush" colors will be equally easy (and warmer) to work around. Or consider a sharper pastel – lilac is sometimes a popular color for bathrooms and can be the basis for a really elegant scheme.

Many bathroom sanitaryware producers have a marketing arrangement with ceramic wall and floor tile manufacturers, so it is fairly easy to find tiles to coordinate well with the ceramic pieces if you want a more subtle scheme. Bear in mind that the tiles and the sanitaryware will be with you for a long time to come, so do some very careful

sampling before reaching a decision. If the tiles are patterned, make sure that the overall effect will not be too overpowering in a small space – or that the design will not appear to be sliding off the wall when completely tiled! Look at as many tiles side by side as possible; pictures and leaflets are also useful as a guide to the overall effect, but do not rely on them for accurate color matching.

If a bathroom and bedroom are *en suite*, aim to create a visual link between the two rooms. Carry some color through from the bedroom into the bathroom (or vice versa)

with the same, or a similar color, on the floor; choose a patterned (or a coordinating) fabric for curtains in the bedroom and blinds in the bathroom; echo the color of the bathroom wall tiles in the bedroom wall treatment, perhaps using matching borders in both areas; and pick accessories which also relate to both schemes.

The Bedroom

Bedrooms are usually highly personal spaces. In addition to being used for sleeping, changing clothes, etc., and as a private area in which to relax

away from the rest of the family, they provide storage space for personal possessions. In some cases a bedroom may double as a study, workroom or playroom – as well as being somewhere to sleep.

Most bedrooms can be colored, styled, decorated and furnished in a more individual way than the communal areas of the home, although shared spaces (master bedroom, childrens' rooms) need very careful furnishing and styling to satisfy all the occupants.

The first essential item is a comfortable bed, which can be

◄ Two tones of glazed plain wall tiles are hung trellis-fashion to create a dado, bordered with a plain contrasting tile. Coordinating larger floor pavers echo the diamond design on the wall. [Fired Earth]

▼ Plain tiles in contrasting rich, dark and pale, cool colors, grouted in white for greater emphasis, create a sophisticated, individual scheme very simply. [Ann Sacks]

◄◄ This bathroom is completely tiled and floored to coordinate with the elegant fittings. Bathroom floor tiles must always be non-slip. [Ideal Standard]

selected to fit in with your chosen theme – from an opulently draped four-poster or Victorian brass bedstead, to streamlined sofa bed or futon. The choice of bed also depends on the style of the room. If you want it to stand out and dominate, dress it extravagantly to contrast with the floor and wall treatments, although these could link up with the other fabrics in the scheme. If you want it to be self-effacing, cover the bed to blend in with the surroundings (floor and walls).

Adequate storage is the next thing to consider. Whenever possible, plan this from the inside out, figuring out exactly what you need to store, and designing cupboards and units around personal requirements. For free-standing furniture, check interior as well as exterior measurements to make sure it will hold all the things you need to put in it. Check the depth and bases of drawers, as well as ease of opening and the strength of runners to be sure they will not collapse. For a more traditional theme, a Victorian or Edwardian washstand with a tiled or marble top can hold the conventional "jug-and-basin" set, or be used as a practical dressing table surface, or even be adapted to take a plumbed-in basin. Old wooden-topped dressing tables and washstands can be tiled with a suitable ceramic tile, although the framework may need strengthening to take the extra weight. Use the type of grouting manufactured for use in the kitchen to be impervious to spillages. This piece could be coordinated into the scheme with a matching tiled splashback.

Room to Relax
Choose the color scheme and pattern "mix" with relaxation in mind. Avoid strongly contrasting colors and bold patterns unless the room is very light and airy, or you want to set a stimulating scheme for a child. Too many shiny textures,

◀ Large strong-colored tiles with a diamond border show off the all-white fixtures to great effect. [Ideal Standard]

▼ Gleaming white wall tiles have an inset border to outline the bathtub and other features. Coordinating floor tiles draw the eye to the attractive older style, cast-iron tub. [Corres Mexican Tiles]

▶ An all-white bathroom relies on contrast of curving forms and neat geometric tiling for effect. Color accents can be changed to suit the mood – or the season. [Ideal Standard]

especially on walls, can be dazzling, so incorporate delicate light-filtering fabrics, slatted blinds and shutters, lace-trimmed bedlinens and wicker items for a feminine feel and to provide textural contrast.

The lighter values of the cooler colors (lilac, silvers, soft greens, pale blues) will help to create a peaceful mood and will add an impression of light and space. These colors may be too unwelcoming in a cold, dark room, so use soft yellows or warm peach with gold or terracotta, and contrast with sparkling white or subtle creams, accented with sharp blues or glossy greens. Alternatively, use frankly feminine pinks, teamed with sophisticated rose, "cooled" with navy blue, lavender or gray. If these softer shades or sugar-sweet florals are too pretty for a shared

bedroom, look at the sophisticated "true" neutrals – different tones of gray with black and white, and enliven the scheme with a few bright accents. Or perhaps the more "earthy" neutrals might be more appropriate – warm browns and burnt orange, teamed with burlap (hessian)-beige, taupe, ecru, creams, and spiced up with Chinese jade and aqua greens, or lapis-lazuli blues.

Childrens' bedrooms require different considerations. There is plenty of scope for imaginative treatments – colors can be bold, stimulating primaries, or use the slightly softer sugared-almond colors. There are many specialist designs available on wallcoverings, borders, tiles, bedding, fabrics and accessories, but you can create your own scene with murals, stencils, posters, etc.

Remember that children soon tire of current fads and outgrow nursery, film or television characters even more quickly than they do child-sized furniture!

Teenagers' rooms can be more sophisticated, with subtle middle-tone shades chosen to suit the owner and their particular interests – for instance, "racing" green teamed with terracotta; the favorite football team's colors; black, deep blue with gray and white, decorated with silver stars; the more feminine pinks, lilacs and mauves associated with ballet, etc. Whatever scheme you select for such rooms, choose practical, washable surfaces for floors and walls.

A Different Dimension
Most bedrooms have plenty of richly textured curtains and soft furnishings

which create a gentle, welcoming mood. These can be emphasized and contrasted with tiled and other hard flooring, particularly in a dual-purpose bedroom and playroom. Rugs (non-slip) can provide under-foot comfort on cooler days, especially if the theme is minimalist, country style, colorful Mediterranean, or eclectic ethnic. They are also good to use where children indulge in messy play.

Ceramic tiles can also be used for splashbacks on walls behind any basin or dressing table, and make a really practical surface treatment in a baby-changing area. The harsh texture of the basin and tiles can be offset with a frilled or pleated fabric valance, perhaps in fabric to match the window treatment, and attached to hide the pipework or table legs.

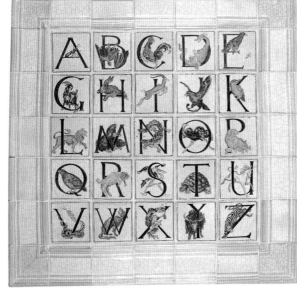

◀ A raised four-tile fish panel in soft colors provides a focus above the faucet. [Ann Sacks]

▲ Alphabet tiles, set here as a decorative panel above a baby-changing area, can be used as a border or insets in almost any room. [Country Floors]

▶ Blue and white floral tiles above a bedroom sink area frame the mirrors, linking them with the walls and counters to create a sparkling effect. [Société Carré]

COLOR
DIRECTORY

USING COLOR AND PATTERN – THE BASICS

When designing, refurbishing, decorating or furnishing any room, there are certain basic principles to consider; and four allies to help you achieve stunning results – color, pattern, texture and form.

Color helps to create a mood or ambience, and can suggest a specific traditional flavor. Colors can be combined for a stimulating or a relaxing effect. They can be used to warm up cold areas and to cool down hot ones. Color can create space visually and introduce a feeling of cozy intimacy.

Patterns can set the style of a room, as well as provide visual interest. Certain designs used on major surfaces will set a modern or authentic period look. Pattern, like color, can be used to help adjust the visual proportions of a room. They can both be used to emphasize good features and play down ugly ones.

Texture exists on every surface – some are shiny and light-reflecting, and others are matte, flat and light-absorbing. Sculpted, rough and rustic textures rely on the play of light across their surface for maximum effect, while light-filtering ones diffuse the light. Textures in turn relate to the color on the surface – making it brighter (light-reflecting), darker or duller (light-absorbing), or more fragile and delicate (light-filtering). Contrast in texture is essential to a successful scheme.

Form, or shape, is another important "ingredient." It can be square or oblong and angular, linear, softly flowing, or rounded and curvaceous. Aim for a balance of forms in a room, combining several different shapes on both the horizontal and vertical planes.

Color Theory
There are three basic types of color – warm, cool and neutral.
Warm advancing colors can warm up a space or create a cozy feel in a large room. Because they appear to come forwards, they can be enclosing, especially in their brighter versions. Examples are red-violet, red, red-orange, orange, yellow-orange, yellow, some yellow-greens, and all their different values (strength or weight of color) from palest pink, lemon, peach and apricot to deep wine reds, glowing golds and earthy terracottas.

Cool receding colors in their palest values create an impression of cool elegance and space as they seem to go away from you. They can be used to cool down a hot or very sunny room. However, brighter versions of cool colors can be demanding. Examples are violets, blue-violets, blue, blue-green, greens and some yellow-greens – and their different tints, tones and shades, from palest lavender and misty sky blues to deepest forest and olive greens. On the color wheel, the warm (advancing) colors are on one side, and on the other are the cool (receding) ones.

Neutrals are the colors which do not appear on the color wheel. They are used to link, contrast, or help to define a color scheme. Neutrals can be used as a background color, although they can be very effective on their own, especially where a minimalist or simple relaxing mood is required. The "true" neutrals are black, white and pure gray. Gray is made by mixing white and black together, and depending on the proportions used, can range from pale silver to deep charcoal. There are also "accepted" neutrals – cream, off-white, beige and the colors of natural materials. Many "accepted" neutrals have cool, receding or warm, advancing qualities.

Color Harmonizing
It is, of course, the way colors are used together that gives a room mood, character and style. There are several accepted ways of color scheming called "color harmonies" – although they are not necessarily harmonious! To create a balanced color scheme, it is essential to have tonal contrast, achieved by introducing different strengths (or values) of color.

A **complementary color scheme** uses colors opposite each other on the color wheel – red and green, orange and blue, lilac and yellow – in all their tonal variations. For example, pale pink and forest green, terracotta and turquoise, mauve and gold are all complementary schemes. As these schemes combine a warm, advancing color with a cool, receding one, the effect is usually dramatic.

An **adjacent color scheme** is when "neighborly" colors (next to each other on the color wheel) are used together. Several segments – two, three, four or five – can make up the scheme. When the blues and greens are used, the effect is cool; warm adjacent neighbors (yellow, gold and burnt orange) create a cozy feel. Either "mix" is more relaxing than a complementary scheme. A combination of cool and warm colors next to each other is more stimulating – for example, blue, green, yellow-greens, yellow or orange with magenta, lilac, blue and blue-green.

A **monochromatic color scheme** (sometimes called a tone-on-tone scheme) uses different values (strengths) of one color. It is essential to use different tones of color to avoid a bland and boring scheme. It also helps to contrast such schemes with a suitable neutral and to introduce a strong accent color in accessories, taken from the opposite side of the color wheel. When choosing glazed ceramic tiles, remember that the color will often look much brighter or stronger *en masse* due to the light reflecting off the surface. Patterns can be surprisingly deceptive, especially if you have only seen a single tile.

Picking Patterns
As with warm and cool colors, patterns can be advancing or receding. Bold geometric, floral and regular repeating designs tend to advance and so look stronger when spread over a large floor, wall or window area. Such bold effects are best used in big rooms where they can be fully appreciated. Small patterns work like receding colors, having a tendency to fade into insignificance when spread over a large surface. They are best used in smaller rooms or where a feeling of space is required. It is essential to relate the strength of the color and the boldness of the pattern to the size of the surface – they should always be in the correct scale.

In most supplier's and manufacturer's collections you will find a wide range of colors, patterns, styles and textures. One exciting way to use colorful tiles is to create a patch-work pattern – but make sure that the tiles are of the same depth and strength. [Société Carré]

It can be difficult to relate a small sample or only one tile to the finished effect on a whole wall or floor. Illustrations in leaflets, pattern books or on packaging can give an impression of how the design works, but never put your trust in them for color-matching. Always try to see as large a sample as possible of any fabrics, wallcovering or paint, etc., and on the correct plane. Gather fabric for curtains/shades in your hand to get a more accurate idea of how it will look when made.

Group several tiles together (especially if they are patterned) so you can see how the design "travels" across the surface. Some suppliers display wall tiles mounted on pull-out boards and floor tiles in drawers, or in special mirrored boxes so you can judge the effect more easily. If you are not offered any of these displays, you may have to open a box and set out some of the tiles on a flat surface.

Color and patterns for tiles, bathroom fixtures, kitchen units and work surfaces need to be very carefully considered since they are all semi-permanent fixtures and will probably have several schemes worked around them during their lifetime, so try to plan ahead. This is equally true of the floor. All the tiles and slabs in this book are classed as hard floorings and become a permanent part of the structure of a room once they are installed. So again, when deciding on design and choosing color, think about the need to plan future color schemes.

Professional interior designers plan a scheme from the floor up, unless there is already an existing limitation in the room. Almost everything in the room is seen in relation to it – walls and woodwork (baseboard [skirting], doors) butt up to it; drapes and curtains touch it; furniture, appliances and equipment "sit" on it. So bear all these things in mind when choosing flooring.

Finally, never underestimate the importance of color "sampling." Always obtain adequately sized samples of any proposed materials (at least one tile, preferably several) and look at them in the room where you propose to use them under *exact lighting conditions* – both in daylight and night (artificial) light.

ROSY
REDS

RICH REDS AND PURPLES ARE VIBRANT AND EXCITING. THEY
ARE THE STRONGEST OF THE ADVANCING COLORS AND
CAN BE USED TO DECREASE THE SIZE OF A ROOM
VISUALLY AND MAKE IT SEEM MORE WELCOMING
AND COZY. PALER PINKS AND VIOLETS
ARE SHADES OF SENSUALITY,
WELL-BEING AND ENCHANTMENT.
RED'S COMPLEMENTARY
COLOR IS GREEN;
PURPLE'S IS
YELLOW.

RED
TILE
DIRECTORY

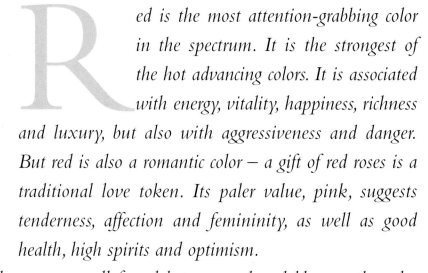

ed is the most attention-grabbing color in the spectrum. It is the strongest of the hot advancing colors. It is associated with energy, vitality, happiness, richness and luxury, but also with aggressiveness and danger. But red is also a romantic color – a gift of red roses is a traditional love token. Its paler value, pink, suggests tenderness, affection and femininity, as well as good health, high spirits and optimism.

Purple, violet and mauve are all found between red and blue on the color wheel, where the warm and cool colors meet. A purple can therefore be warm or cool. These colors represent sensitivity, knowledge, sanctity, humility, nostalgia and sorrow. Strong purple radiates self-esteem and confidence. Violet is the color of Mary Magdalene and the god Jupiter. The paler mauves and violets are

the shades of sensuality and enchantment, and are linked with good taste and an appreciation of the arts, music, philosophy and ballet.

Bold reds appear to come towards you and can be used to make a space look smaller, warmer and more welcoming. A cold bathroom with clinical-looking white equipment and tiles can be made much more user-friendly with a subtle pink and rose red color scheme. However, if the brighter values of red are used indiscriminately, they can induce a claustrophobic and over-stimulating sensation. A scheme incorporating strong

alues of red and green (the complementary of red) will be very stimulating and best used in areas where you want to discourage lingering, such as a family bathroom or a cold, bleak hall.

Like red, purple in its strongest value is vibrant and demanding, and can therefore be overpowering, so it needs to be contrasted with pastel colors or subtle neutrals. A tone-on-tone scheme of purples and violets with white, black and gray will set a modern, sophisticated scene in a formal room – especially one with a Gothic flavor, where the black accents can be provided in wrought-iron fixtures. The slightly gray or plum tones of reddish-purple are warm and inviting, and look very elegant in the right setting – for instance, an imposing hall, a formal dining room or an opulent bedroom, especially in an older-style property.

Lilac has long been a forgotten color but is coming back into its own, particularly in the bathroom. It is also a surprisingly effective, but rarely used, color for a kitchen – lilac wall tiles and a deeper gray-purple on the floor can be the perfect foil for dark spruce green units, or Shaker green free-standing kitchen furniture.

The adjacent colors to purple are blue on one side of the color wheel and red on the other. Blue-purples and violets are wonderfully refreshing when teamed with blues and greens – a good combination for a warm kitchen or sunny conservatory. When mixed with the warmer neighbors (reds and pinks), the effect can be very cozy.

Mexican handmade, hand-decorated glazed tiles
These tiles are shaped to fit around a hand basin which has been decorated to match with a stylized floral motif. [Corres Mexican Tiles]

Brazilian glazed ceramic wall tiles
The deep red field tiles look wonderful with this mosaic-style border. The different shades of blue, together with the bright white grout, have a cooling effect. [Shelly]

French handmade glazed wall tiles
These bright pink tiles are topped with a traditional raised leaf border in white and framed underneath with a solid red liner. The central diamonds are in white and red, demonstrating the different effects which can be achieved with such a simple change of color. [Elon]

Moroccan handmade floor tiles
These are made from stone, marble and white cement mix using the traditional encaustic method. The pattern is created by using plain tiles laid diamond-fashion, finished with surrounding borders to create the look of a decorative rug. [Carreaux de Casbah]

"Red" tiles range from palest pink, through dusky rose to scarlet. When floral designs are used with this color, the effect is simply stunning. [l to r: Country Floors (a, b, c), Hastings (d, f), Carreaux de Casbah (e)]

Italian glazed wall tiles

These frostproof tiles have jewel-bright motifs framed within a red background and scatter patterns of red, white, black and blue. Experiment by teaming them with solid white or black tiles to produce starkly different effects. [Hastings]

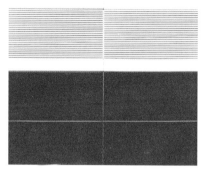

Italian matte-glazed wall tiles

A subtle horizontal effect is created by combining pink, red and white – an effective treatment to widen a narrow wall area visually with plain tiles. [Hastings]

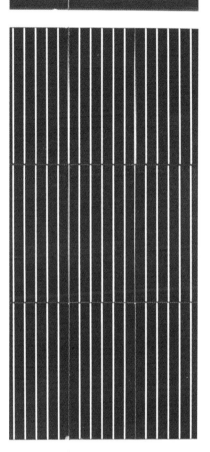

Italian glazed wall tiles

Modern abstract patterns used as a whole tile or as a border to a solid white center create a bright and cheerful effect. The two dominant colors in the designs are red and yellow, so coordinate with plain tiles in these colors to create unusual effects. [Hastings]

Italian glazed wall tiles

The solid colors and random stripe create a stylish treatment. Use this type of tile design only on level, perfectly square walls or they could appear to be slipping off! [Hastings]

Spanish glazed wall tiles

The octagonal-shaped white tiles have bright red square insets dropped in diamond-fashion at the corners and are outlined with a narrow red-and-white diamond pattern and white raised rope border to form a stylish splashback or border. [Country Floors]

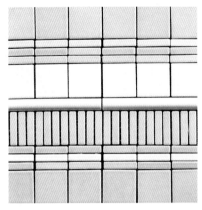

Hand-glazed wall tiles
These deep pinkish-purple tones would look good with matching and coordinating hand basins and patterned tiles. [Elon]

French glazed wall tiles
Abstract-patterned drop-in tiles are teamed with candy-colored purple and green plain tiles. They are ideal for a child's room or a family bathroom. [Ideal Tiles]

Porcelain glazed tiles and liners
These tiles create an attractive textured geometric effect for bathrooms and shower rooms. [Shelly]

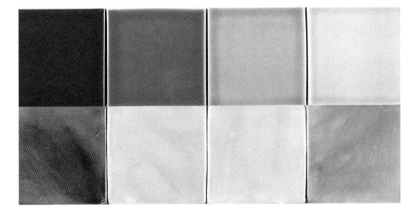

Glazed ceramic wall tiles
These tiles are hand-colored to produce variegated shades of pink. The deeper pink and white liner acts as a link with the pastel blue border. [Hastings]

American handmade, hand-molded, thickly-glazed wall tiles
Use these for bathroom, kitchen and utility areas with coordinating borders, relief nosings and other shapes. The rich colors go right through the spectrum from pale pink to deep bluish-purple and would warm up the coldest bathroom. [Country Floors]

Italian textured earthenware tiles
In wonderful jewel-rich colors and ethnic patterns, these tiles can be combined to create panels, splashbacks, borders, frames, etc. The seashore theme makes them ideal for a bathroom but they would need sealing with a penetrating sealer, preferably before hanging, as they would not be waterproof in a shower situation. [Ann Sacks]

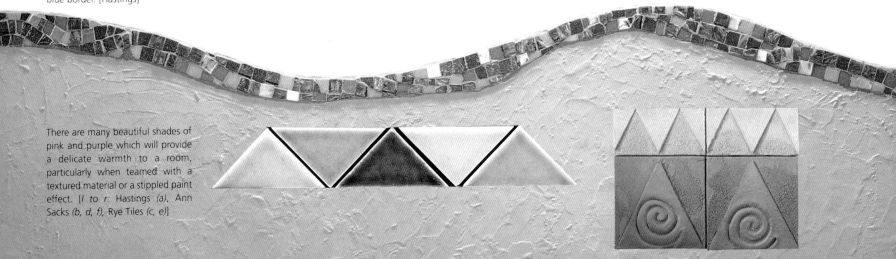

There are many beautiful shades of pink and purple which will provide a delicate warmth to a room, particularly when teamed with a textured material or a stippled paint effect. [l to r: Hastings (a), Ann Sacks (b, d, f), Rye Tiles (c, e)]

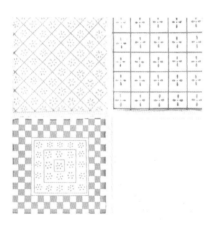

French glazed ceramic wall tiles

Gingham checks and mini-geometrics in clear pink are hand-painted on a white ground. These tiles can be used to create a patchwork pattern, and/or mixed with plain pink or white field tiles. [Ideal Tiles]

Glazed ceramic wall tiles

Different modules can be used to build up a wall panel. The central row of square tiles are bordered by quarter-size white tiles and then a floral border. The different-sized tiles add extra visual interest. Although the central row of tiles is primarily blue, the softest hint of graduated red tones are added to introduce a subtle but effective warmth to the design. [Shelly]

Hand-painted glazed wall tiles

This bunch of luscious eggplants look as though they are hanging from a pine strip. Make a decorative panel with three of them or use them as single features. [Country Floors]

Italian textured earthenware tiles

The rich shades of purple are combined with ethnic patterns to create a stunning panel. The desert theme of the tiles makes them ideal for a conservatory or bathroom. [Ann Sacks]

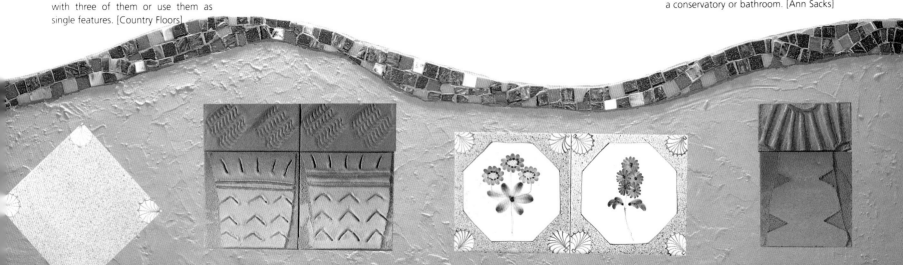

Glazed ceramic and terracotta tiles

Dramatic effect is created with a combination of different-sized tiles in subtle Arts & Crafts glazes. They can be used on floors (light use), countertops, for fireplaces and stoves, as wall panels and dados. The reddish glaze is stronger on the outer border, thus drawing more attention to the lighter central area. [Ann Sacks]

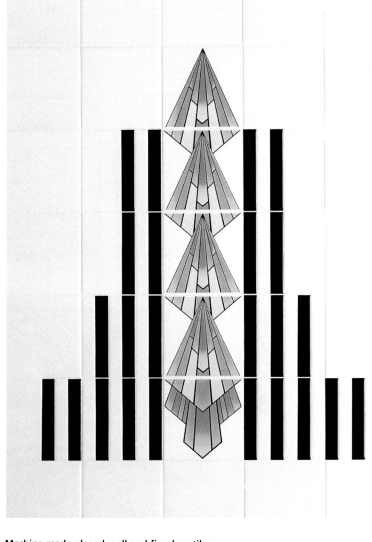

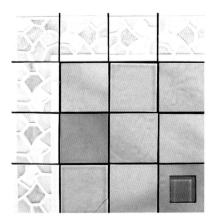

Brazilian hand-painted glazed wall tiles

A 50's abstract pattern is used as a border to enclose a panel of plain-colored tiles with a bold purple contrasting square. [Shelly]

French ceramic wall tiles

Pastel pink and gray-green tiles look attractive in bathrooms. The ridged diamond patterns on the liners have a handcrafted look, further emphasized by the thick white grout and the combination of tile shapes. [Shelly]

Machine-made glazed wall and fireplace tiles

This authentic Art Deco design is based on established patterns of the period. Soft pinks and lilacs are combined with black and gray for a sophisticated scheme. The different tiles can be used to build up a panel; form fireplace columns; outline a feature; make a decorative dado rail – ideal in an Edwardian hall. [Minton Hollins]

Muted shades of pink bear a strong affinity to terracotta and have the same warmth. They are beautiful as plain tiles laid in geometric designs or teamed with floral patterns. [*l to r:* Ann Sacks *(a, c, e)*, Country Floors *(b)*, Carreaux de Casbah *(d)*, Elon Tiles *(f)*]

Spanish handmade terracotta tiles

Suitable for floors and walls, these plain tiles are surrounded by a stunning mosaic border made up of a spectrum of colors. The tiles are porous and therefore need a penetrating sealer [Ann Sacks]

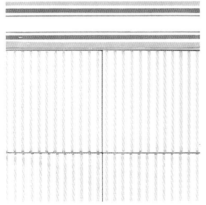

Italian glazed wall and floor tiles

These stylish minimalist stripes in clear red on white can be combined with a coordinating horizontal striped border when used on walls. [Country Floors]

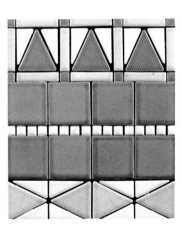

Glazed ceramic tiles

The upper row of pink and white triangles would look good as drop-ins amongst turquoise tiles; the lower row would form an attractive border on a plain wall area. [Shelly]

Handcrafted, rustic molded tiles

This fan frieze with ram's head insets has a Gothic flavor and makes a perfect border for a fireplace. It could also be used on walls and exterior façades. [Ann Sacks]

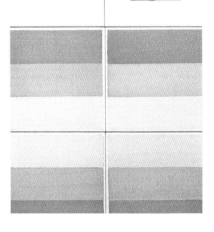

Italian glazed wall tiles

These tiles have blocked and striped color geometric effects in monochromatic tones on white. Mix and match them to create unusual patterned effects with what are virtually plain tiles. [Hastings]

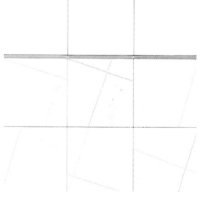

Italian glazed wall tiles

The slanting abstract pattern in soft pink links with the neat deeper pink edging on the border tile, ideal for bathroom walls. [Hastings]

Hand-decorated glazed wall tiles
The floral patterns are combined with plain coordinating red color-wash tiles to create a checkerboard-effect wall panel. [Shelly]

Antiqued relief-patterned glazed tiles
The grapes and vine leaves are in warm earth colors and frame a panel of coordinating field tiles. They can be used to form borders, panels, patterns or as drop-ins on walls, or around stoves and fireplaces. [Ann Sacks]

Glazed ceramic wall tiles
From deep crimson to peony pink, red-toned tiles make the perfect surround for a fireplace, enhancing the warmth of the room. These field tiles, liners and floral-patterned drop-ins have a traditional appeal. [Shelly]

Spanish glazed clay tiles
The red floral border has a purple stripe around it to help distinguish the liners from the central panel of tiles. A colored grout would have the same effect. [Ann Sacks]

Hand-painted matte-glazed tiles
These tiles build up to form a daisy mural of colorful flowers which spring from a coordinating jug. The softly flowing leaf border echos the leaves in the bouquet. The panel would be an eye-catching focal point in a plain tiled wall, or pretty as a splashback in a windowless area. [Ann Sacks]

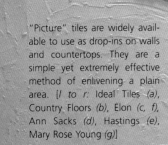

"Picture" tiles are widely available to use as drop-ins on walls and countertops. They are a simple yet extremely effective method of enlivening a plain area. [l to r: Ideal Tiles (a), Country Floors (b), Elon (c, f), Ann Sacks (d), Hastings (e), Mary Rose Young (g)]

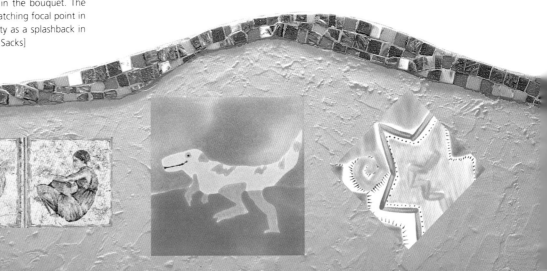

Glazed ceramic wall tiles
This picture panel has been treated to produce a handcrafted look. The autumnal fruits and leaves with blackbird border make this ideal for a kitchen, particularly one without a view. [Ann Sacks]

Screen-printed glazed wall tiles
These have a flowing floral design in pinks and greens on a soft white ground. Twelve tiles form a panel with the bolder bouquet spreading across the central tiles. [Caroline & Stephen Atkinson-Jones]

Hand-decorated heatproof glazed tiles
These Victorian-style tiles can be used to form panels, borders, dados, etc., but can also be used as paneled insets for fireplaces to create a traditional look. [Acquisitions]

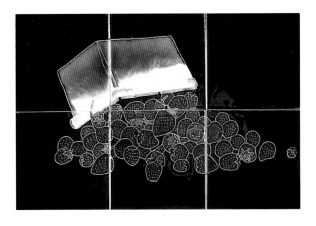

American glazed wall tiles
These are decorated to depict a basket of luscious strawberries – ideal for kitchens, dining rooms or appropriate commercial situations. [Hastings]

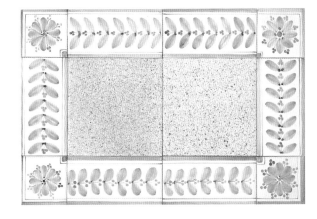

Hand-decorated glazed wall tiles
This tiled panel is suitable for bathrooms, showers, kitchens or fireplaces. It could be used effectively above a sink, bath or stove, or as an interesting feature on a blank wall. The border tiles can be used to top a splashback or create a dado rail. [Rye Tiles]

VIBRANT
ORANGES

ORANGE IS ONE OF THE WARMEST COLORS. THE BOLD
VALUES ARE ALMOST AS INTENSE AND AS ADVANCING
AS RED, AND IN NATURE THEY ARE TEMPERED
WITH COOL COLORS. THE PALER, MORE
SUBTLE ORANGE TINTS AND TONES
ARE WARM AND WELCOMING,
AND ACT AS A "SUNSHINE"
COLOR. ITS
COMPLEMENTARY
COLOR IS
BLUE.

ORANGE

TILE DIRECTORY

Orange is one of the warmest colors — the bold values are strident, domineering and almost as intense and advancing as red. The paler and more subtle tints and tones — such as peach, apricot, melon and terracotta — are warm and welcoming and, like yellow, act as a "sunshine" color. Orange is also the color of the earth; deep orange-brown clays are used to make floor and wall tiles; copper and bronze are both orange with a metallic luster; and gemstones include topaz, amber and citrine quartz. In nature the color is found in exotic birds, butterflies and fish; summer flowerbeds are radiant with orange flowers, and autumn is ablaze with the variety of tones in the changing foliage and harvest fruits.

Orange combines the physical energy of red with the intellect of yellow — the two hues mixed together create pure orange. In heraldry orange symbolizes strength and endurance, and in Greek mythology it was associated with Zeus, ruler of the gods. In Buddhism orange suggests humility — hence the saffron robes (it was also the dress color for the humble in earlier times; for example, clerks wore orange-tawny). To the Chinese and Japanese, it is the color of love and happiness. In Europe orange is a color of temptation: paintings depict Eve seducing Adam with an orange or a peach instead of an apple. Auburn hair is also synonymous with the temptress — the romantic heroines of Pre-Raphaelite paintings have long, thick, auburn

hair, and in Ancient Rome women hennaed their hair to please their husbands. Bold orange is very stimulating, so it is wise to confine strong tones to the smaller surfaces in a room, or use it for accents or as part of an overall patterned surface. When orange is teamed with its complementary color blue, or combined with black or gray and white, it is best used for rooms not intended for relaxation — for example, playrooms.

In nature, the more fiery oranges are nearly always tempered with cool green foliage, set against a clear blue or misty gray sky, or perhaps seen in relation to rich earthy browns or natural stone and wood. These are all good color combinations to bring indoors to create an elegant atmosphere of warmth and welcome. Subtle shades of burnt orange or chestnut teamed with creamy beige and bright blue are the traditional colors of Victorian encaustic tiled floors. With this color range shifted up a gear to strong orange, Madonna blue, jade and ocher with crisp white, a Mediterranean ambience is suggested.

The bolder and darker values of orange also need some neutral touches, as well as color contrasts, to use them to full advantage. Black, white and gray work well with the terracotta tones — an "Etruscan" combination very popular in the seventeenth and eighteenth centuries and evocative of Josiah Wedgwood's Jasperware. Such color schemes are elegant and inviting, but can also seem enclosing. The paler tones — e.g. peach or apricot — create a more relaxed, natural theme and may also need neutral touches and balancing with rich chestnut or dark, warm browns.

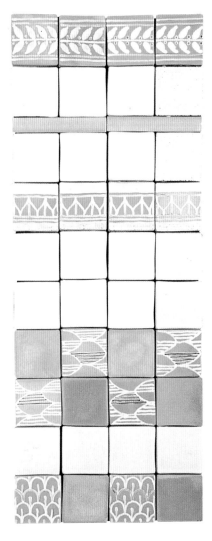

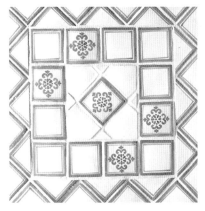

Mexican handmade, hand-painted glazed wall tiles

Use these to drop in as insets, or to form a feature panel. [Corres Mexican Tiles]

Hand-decorated glazed wall tiles

Inspired by Islamic decoration and William Morris florals of the Victorian era, here soft terracotta is used with its complement blue. Many permutations and other color combinations could be used to create different traditional effects. [Sally Anderson Ceramics]

Glazed ceramic wall tiles

A clean, summery look is achieved with soft apricot and plain white tiles. Here, a patterned border and drop-in tiles are highlighted with touches of blue and yellow. [Hastings]

Portuguese hand-painted glazed ceramic wall tiles

The traditional floral motif forms a geometric pattern when hung as a splashback, panel or dado. The single motif tile could be used as a border to finish a plain tiled area, in a coordinating color. [Ideal Tiles]

French faience-glazed wall tiles

These tiles can be combined with plain field tiles to form a dado effect for bathrooms, kitchens, utility rooms, conservatories, halls, etc. The overall effect of this dahlia design is of a flower-filled windowbox. [Ceramique Internationale]

Plain terracotta tiles are ideal where an earthy, rustic look is required. They are attractive as a backdrop for pictorial drop-ins and borders as well as for use in geometric designs. [l to r: Country Floors (a), Corres Mexican Tiles (b, d), Carreaux de Casbah (c), Ann Sacks (e), Elon Tiles (f), Sussex Terracotta (g)]

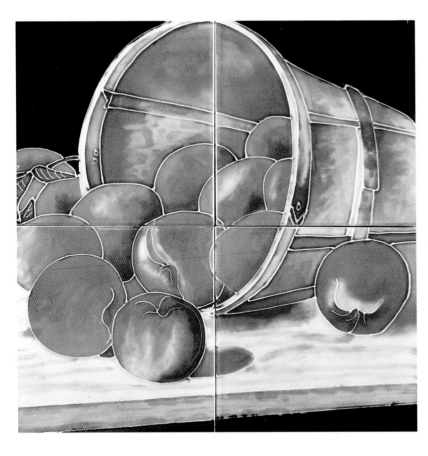

Hand-decorated glazed tiles
These tiles depict autumnal-colored fruit, tumbling out of a rustic basket, ideal for kitchen sink/countertop splashbacks or behind stoves. [Hastings]

Mexican handcut, hand-decorated glazed wall tiles
The central pure white tiles are set diamond-fashion inside the blue-orange border for extra visual interest. [Corres Mexican Tiles]

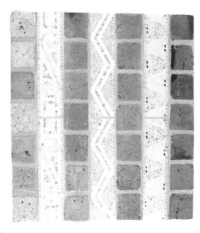

Handmade mosaic border tiles
The scroll, chevron or wave pattern can be set into a terracotta floor to create a decorative design – ideal for floors where the mosaic border can outline features or define the shape of the area. [Marston & Langinger]

Hand-decorated clay wall tiles
Plain tiles are interspersed with brightly colored picture tiles and contrasting turquoise blue liner, ideal for a child's room or bathroom. [Hastings]

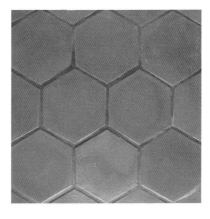

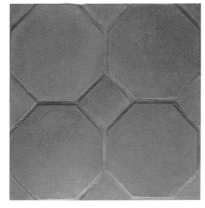

Unglazed terracotta floor tiles
These hexagonal tiles are used without inserts to form a classic patchwork pattern; they are handmade from Barro clay for a warm, natural surface. [Corres Mexican Tiles]

Handmade unglazed terracotta floor tiles
The characteristic burnt orange color can be combined with insert tiles in self-color to build up a traditional geometric pattern. [Corres Mexican Tiles]

Handmade unglazed terracotta floor tiles
In warm burnt orange, square tiles are enclosed by interlocking lozenge-shaped tiles to create a classic geometric design. [Corres Mexican Tiles]

Handmade unglazed terracotta floor tiles
Square tiles are laid diamond-fashion and bordered with same-size square tiles to create a traditional geometric effect. Plain tiles can be used in many ways to create a design without actually being patterned. [Corres Mexican Tiles]

Handmade reclaimed terracotta floor tiles
These are laid brick fashion, with patterned drop-ins to provide extra color and pattern interest. Oblong tiles can be used to create herringbone patterns, to form borders or define areas. [Terra Firma]

Terracotta tiles are extremely popular and are available in a wide range of shapes as they are most commonly used to create geometric or traditional brick patterns for floors. [l to r: Corres Mexican Tiles (a, b, c, d, e), Ann Sacks (f, g)]

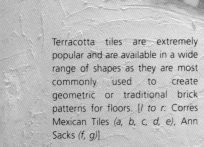

Italian glazed clay floor tiles
This subtle stenciled/batik look is ideal for kitchen floors and countertops. They would make an ideal border to either a plain or patterned floor. [Hastings]

American inlaid terracotta floor tiles
The traditional geometric pattern in subtle blue complements the characteristic orange. These tiles can be laid checkerboard-fashion with plain terracotta field tiles, or as an elegant border. [Country Floors]

Glazed quarry tiles
A patchwork of blue and terracotta tiles is bordered by crosses in a circular design to produce a Gothic look. These tiles are suitable for walls and work surfaces. [Ann Sacks]

Glazed quarry tiles
Suitable for use on walls and countertops, this wonderful Gothic pattern has rich, exciting color combinations. [Ann Sacks]

Glazed wall tiles
These tiles are combined with checkerboard and star liner tiles and a ridged cornice to form an elegant, traditional decorative dado treatment. [Ann Sacks]

Handmade unglazed terracotta floor tiles
These tiles are set out to form a traditional geometric pattern with deep-colored liners and bright insets. [Sussex Terracotta]

Glazed quarry tiles
Deep reds and rustic terracotta are offset with a blue patterned border to produce a distinctive Arts & Crafts flavor. The tiles are suitable for walls or countertops. [Ann Sacks]

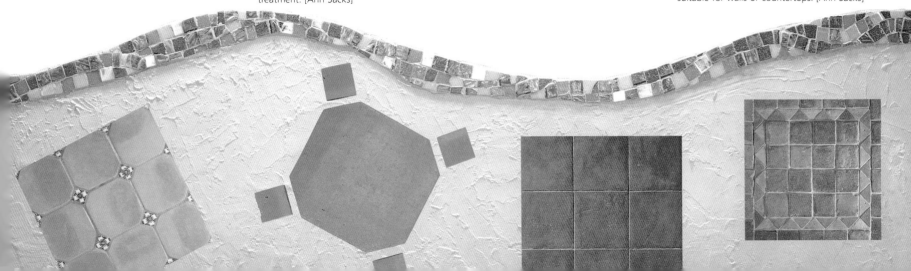

SUNSHINE
YELLOWS

YELLOW IS THE COLOR OF THE SUN'S LIFE-GIVING RAYS.
IT WILL BRING A FEELING OF SUNSHINE, WARMTH
AND LIGHT INTO ANY COLD, DARK ROOM.
PALER VALUES CREATE A SENSE OF SPACE,
ESPECIALLY IF USED ON SHINY
TEXTURED SURFACES SUCH
AS GLAZED TILES. ITS
COMPLEMENTARY
COLOR IS VIOLET
OR PURPLE.

YELLOW
TILE
DIRECTORY

Yellow is the color of the sun's life-giving rays and is associated with well-being, intellect and creative energy. Yellow suggests power, wealth, royalty, privilege and pageantry (being the color of the medieval "field of the cloth of gold") and in heraldry it symbolizes honor and loyalty.

For Christians and Hindus yellow is the color of life and truth; in ancient Greece and Rome it represented the arts and learning and was the color of Athena, goddess of wisdom.

Yellow is also closely associated with nature – it is the warm welcoming color of spring flowers emerging after winter's gloom, from palest primrose to eye-stopping daffodil. The clear sunshine yellows, sand golds and sunflowers associated with summer and the blue sky can all be contrasted with the rich, glowing golds and bronzes of autumn foliage and harvest.

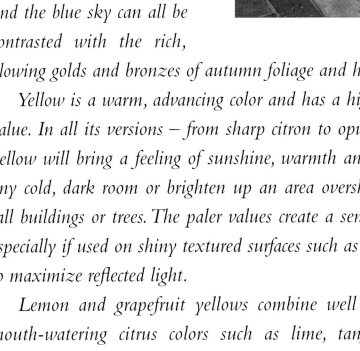

Yellow is a warm, advancing color and has a high reflective value. In all its versions – from sharp citron to opulent gold – yellow will bring a feeling of sunshine, warmth and light into any cold, dark room or brighten up an area overshadowed by tall buildings or trees. The paler values create a sense of space, especially if used on shiny textured surfaces such as glazed tiles to maximize reflected light.

Lemon and grapefruit yellows combine well with other mouth-watering citrus colors such as lime, tangerine and persimmon to create a related scheme in a kitchen or bathroom.

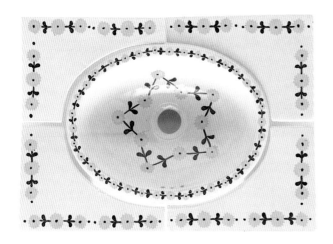

Or clear yellows mixed with the sweet-pea and freesia colors of magenta, mauve, lilac and pink, sparked with white, create a romantic mood in a bedroom.

Exciting effects can be made by contrasting warm advancing colors with cool receding ones — for example, the warmth of yellow balanced with glossy leaf greens is a combination often seen in nature; think of daffodils or sunflowers. There are numerous such combinations for different effects, and the warm color always appears dominant. To achieve a 50/50 balance, use one-third warm yellow to two-thirds cold contrast. Yellow also works well on its own in a tone-on-tone color scheme as long as there is plenty of tonal and textural contrast.

The complementary color of yellow is lilac, violet or purple, and when used together this combination can be visually very stimulating. The tones should therefore be varied to create a more subtle effect — for instance, pale primrose yellow with bluish-purples and deep gold and touches of brass with lavender.

In a large unwelcoming hall, daunting drawing room or big baronial building, yellow can be mixed with other warm, advancing colors to create an atmosphere of cozy intimacy. When used with deep terracotta, Indian red, wine and strong fuchsia pinks — or even scarlet — yellow will provide the light relief to a bold, exciting scheme. Such rich combinations need off-setting with a neutral color, or when mixed with black and burnished mahogany brown, it creates a sophisticated Regency, Empire or Egyptian theme.

Hand-decorated glazed wall tile

This tile looks like a traditional Delft-style panel. It is edged with a narrow slip border and corner insets in the background color, with contrasting brush line detail, to work as a drop-in or feature tile. [Jones's Tiles]

Hand-decorated glazed wall tiles

A 12-tile panel of floral motif tiles is built up to suggest a spring field full of bright yellow daffodils; the border tiles could be used to top a splashback panel of plain tiles. [Caroline & Stephen Atkinson-Jones]

Handmade, hand-painted glazed wall tiles

Combined with an off-white plain field tile, these tiles build up to form a decorative bright yellow and green daffodil pattern which looks like a springtime window box. Use this type of tile design to create panels, splashbacks or as an important feature in a dark, cold, sunless room. Glazed ceramic tiles are light-reflecting, and yellow is a particularly good color to use to create a feeling of space and light. [Country Tile Design]

Glazed wall tiles

The central 9-tile panel forms a country-style pitcher filled with yellow flowers. Here it is combined with six culinary border tiles. [World's End Tiles]

Fruits and flowers in sunny shades of yellow are ideal for both homes and commercial situations such as a restaurant, fruit or health food store. [*l to r*: Decorum Ceramic Studio (a, b), Tiles of Stow (c), Ann Sacks (d), Mary Rose Young (e)]

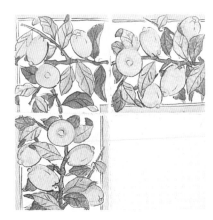

Italian handmade Majolica-glazed terracotta wall tiles

These classic rustic tiles have a lemon-tree border design with matching corner tiles in sharp lemon and green on a white crackle-glaze ground. [Fired Earth]

Portuguese glazed wall and fireplace tiles

These charmingly rustic tiles can also be used on countertops and floors (light use), creating flowing floral patterns. [Ann Sacks]

Portuguese glazed wall and fireplace tiles

These tiles would make a sophisticated border to form a neat finish to wall panels, dados or to frame salient features. [Ann Sacks]

Hand-painted glazed mural wall panel

This six-piece panel creates an authentic botanical look, reminiscent of old prints. It can be used to form an inset panel, or as a frieze. Strong ocher and rose are combined with silvery-green leaves on a cream background. [Corres Mexican Tiles]

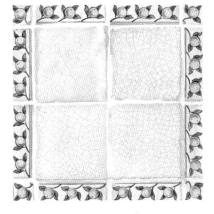

Spanish glazed clay tiles

Ripe fruits form a decorative border around four crackle-glazed tiles which have been treated with a peach colorwash. [Ann Sacks]

Hand-crafted clay wall tiles

This blue-and-yellow floral splashback panel is given added textural interest by the use of raised grouting. [Corres Mexican Tiles]

Italian glazed tiles

This four-tile traditional panel has a strong Mediterranean flavor, suggesting sunshine and warm summer days. The swirling formal pattern will repeat from tile to tile to create a geometric effect. [World's End Tiles]

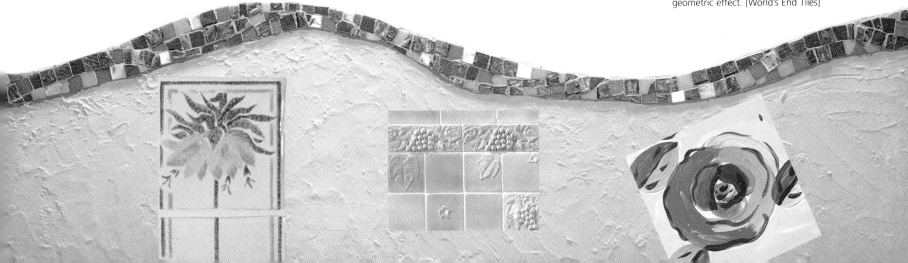

**Italian glazed ceramic
wall tiles**
Solid yellow tiles are laid brick-fashion and enhanced with blue border stripes. [Country Floors]

**Mexican handmade glazed
ceramic wall tiles**
Clear bright colors such as this sunny yellow would cheer up a cold kitchen or bathroom. These tiles can be combined with coordinating patterned ones. [Elon]

American geometric-patterned quarry tiles
In sunshine colors with *cuerda seca*-style glaze, these tiles can be used as borders, inserts and drop-ins to add interest to a plain quarry-tiled floor. [Country Floors]

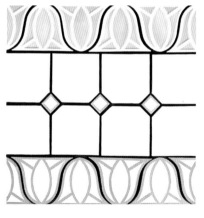

Italian glazed wall tiles
A narrow raised relief diamond border acts as a focus between the square and linear tiles on either side. [Country Floors]

Italian glazed wall tiles
In bright, slightly mottled glaze, these yellow tiles are set diamond-fashion and combined with white diamonds and triangles to form a border with a molded nosing in deep green and blue. [Hastings]

Glazed wall tiles
These Art Nouveau patterned border tiles in yellow and white form a panel with contrasting geometrics and are echoed in a contrasting pink border. [Shelly]

Hand-decorated glazed wall tiles
The all-over repeating pattern of fruit and leaves is reminiscent of Arts & Crafts flowing floral design. Here, nine tiles are used to form a splashback panel. [Jones's Tiles]

Bold, cheerful designs – elephants, circus clowns, flowers and abstract shapes – are a trademark of these yellow tiles, making them particularly useful for a child's room. [*l to r:* Decorum Ceramic Studio (*a, b*), Hastings (*c, d*), Mary Rose Young (*e*)]

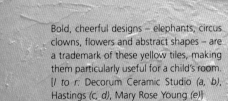

English hand-crafted glazed ceramic wall tiles

These tiles are patterned with yellow frogs on a white ground. Here, two tiles form a panel to show the frog leaping across the seam; however, other amusing leapfrog sequences could be planned. It could be combined with a barleytwist border in coordinating yellow, or contrasting green or dark blue. [Fired Earth]

Handmade, hand-decorated wall panel

These hand-painted glazed tiles have a harvest theme, with glossy wheatsheaf relief; they are ideal for warming up a cold kitchen or for use in a bakery or restaurant. [Country Tile Design]

Spanish handmade terracotta wall tiles

These traditional tiles are glazed in white and hand-decorated with cheerful food and kitchen motifs that can be built up to form an interesting splashback or mural. Here, the design incorporates wine, fruit and fish, ideal for a kitchen or dining room. [Terra Firma]

Hand-painted wall mural

This mural features sunny yellow, cream, strong blue and soft sage greens to make building up a color scheme easier. [Corres Mexican Tiles]

REFRESHING
GREENS

GREEN IS THE COLOR OF NATURE AND SUGGESTS
GROWTH AND REGENERATION. IT IS THE COLOR OF
THE ENVIRONMENTAL MOVEMENT. MOST GREENS
ARE RECEDING AND RESTFUL; THEY CAN
CREATE AN IMPRESSION OF SPACE AND
INTRODUCE A VERDANT FEEL TO
A SUNLESS APARTMENT OR
DRAB BASEMENT. ITS
COMPLEMENTARY
COLOR IS RED.

GREEN
TILE
DIRECTORY

Green is the true color of nature. It is synonymous with foliage, flora, fields and forests, and it suggests growth and regeneration – it is the color of new leaves. Green is always refreshing to look at – a verdant view is excellent relief for tired eyes. In heraldry green is the symbol of hope and growth. It is the sacred color of Islam, and in the Christian church green vestments symbolize the Resurrection and eternal life. The Greeks associated it with Venus, the goddess of love and fertility, and her sacred plant, the evergreen myrtle. The current Green movement strives for the protection of the environment and stands against pollution.

Green is a balancing color; it lies halfway between the warm and cool sections of the color wheel. It can be dark, mysterious, sometimes dangerous (jungle greens); jewel-bright and stimulating (aquamarine, emerald or peridot); cool and elegant as it goes toward its cooler neighbor, blue in the color wheel; and warm and inviting when it is tinged with yellow. Most greens are receding and restful. The paler values can be used to create a calm ambience and an impression of space, and introduce a verdant feel to a sunless city apartment, low-ceilinged attic or drab basement.

Green can be used as an elegant visual link between a garden and a living room, dining room or conservatory. A cool green is a good choice for a kitchen, which is often a hot, steamy center of activity. Forget the old adage "blue and green should never be seen," as a cool, spacious look can

be created using this combination. If strong values of green and red (green is the complementary of red) are used together, the effect can become uncomfortable. More subtle tones of these colors will create a softer effect.

An all-green tone-on-tone scheme appears subtle and spacious but cool and elegant. The palest version could be used on the ceiling, a deeper shade for the walls, a middle tone for the floor, and the deepest value for furniture and perhaps the paintwork. Use a neutral color to link them all and then introduce some warm accessories and accent items. The tonal value and strength of the greens determine the depth of the accent color and should relate to the style of the room.

Combine greens with creamy beige neutrals, natural woods, jute, seagrass and rush matting in a conservatory, country-style kitchen or dining room, cottage bedroom or sitting area — and reintroduce green in foliage plants. Green has always been associated with traditional interiors, particularly those of the Victorian and Edwardian era, when virulent green painted or tiled dados were fashionable. A rich dark green with subtle red can be used to set a Victorian Scottish baronial theme in a large entrance hall, drawing room or study/library. A bold Gothic effect can be created by using "Pugin green" (a clear emerald) with burnt orange, bold cerulean blue and a touch of purple, all offset with black — introduced in the form of wrought-iron light fixtures, curtain poles and finials, and other accessories.

French handmade, hand-painted glazed wall and countertop tiles
This rich "antique" green creates the characteristic rustic look of Normandy in France. [Elon Tiles]

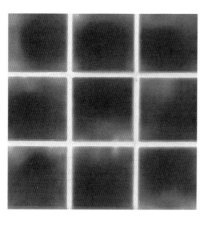

Italian hand-painted glazed wall tiles
Each individual tile has tonal variations, to create a rustic look. [Elon Tiles]

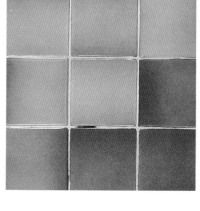

French hand-glazed terracotta wall tiles
The slight color variation is caused by the solid glaze. These tiles can be used on bathroom/bedroom countertops and would look good with a coordinating basin. [Elon]

Mexican handmade terracotta tiles
The solid glaze gives the characteristic dappled look of hand-crafted tiles. These tiles are mainly suitable for walls, although they can be used as colorful drop-ins or key squares in a terracotta tiled floor. [Elon]

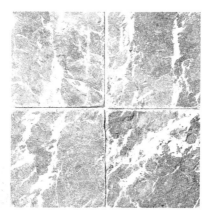

Hand-finished Venetian marble tiles
These can be used on floors and walls for an elegant effect. Take care with marble in a "wet" situation as it can be slippery underfoot. [Metropolitan Tile Company]

Mexican hand-painted glazed wall tiles
Coordinating border tiles and mural panels can be used with these subtly colored tiles to form interesting visual effects. [Elon Tiles]

French hand-glazed terracotta wall tiles
These deep sea green-colored tiles would look superbly refreshing in a bathroom, particularly as a splashback. [Elon]

Mexican handmade glazed wall tiles
Combining the patterned bird and scattered flower motif with richly glazed plain tiles in glorious greens shows how easy tile coordination is. [Corres Mexican Tiles]

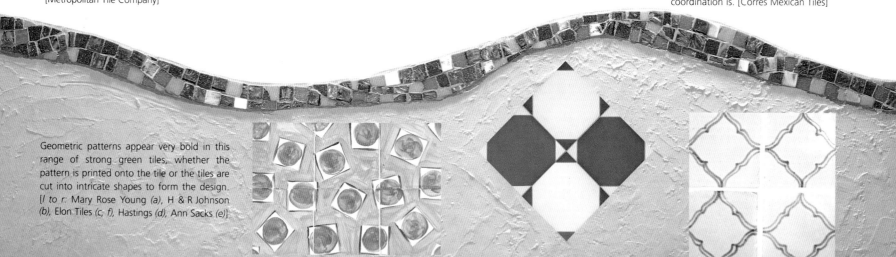

Geometric patterns appear very bold in this range of strong green tiles, whether the pattern is printed onto the tile or the tiles are cut into intricate shapes to form the design. [l to r: Mary Rose Young (a), H & R Johnson (b), Elon Tiles (c, f), Hastings (d), Ann Sacks (e)]

American glazed wall tiles
These octagonal-shaped tiles are combined with insets and bordered with top-cap molding in rich green. [Country Floors]

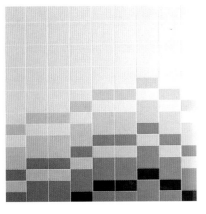

Machine-made vitrified wall tiles
Use these tiles to create a monochromatic scheme in tones of pale aquas through to deep green. The exciting colors allow many innovative design possibilities including cut-tile mural design. [H & R Johnson]

Quarried slate with terracotta insets
These tiles are laid to form a classic key-square effect with a slate border. Use them for floors both indoors and out, but bear in mind that calibrated slate needs sealing with a special sealant. [Ann Sacks]

Riven slate floor tiles
These tiles are set in classical fashion with small corner insets and neat narrow borders. They could be laid across a hall, conservatory, kitchen or living-room floor to create the look of traditional flagstones. [Ann Sacks]

Italian glazed terracotta wall tiles
Pale green tiles border a pink diamond with a coordinating pink-and-white nosing to form a pretty bathroom splashback. [Elon Tiles]

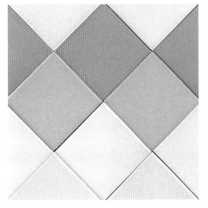

Glazed ceramic wall tiles
This geometric diamond pattern is created with different tones of blue-green which could be used as an interesting dado rail-type border on a wall of white tiles. [Hastings]

Natural quarried slate
Warm green slate is laid in a classic brick pattern. Natural slate is multi-colored and both sides can be used face-up, giving more opportunities for achieving the tonal balance you require. [Ann Sacks]

Riven slate floor tiles
Laid edge-to-edge in brick pattern, the characteristic color variations and slight veining found in natural quarried products is made into a design feature. [Ann Sacks]

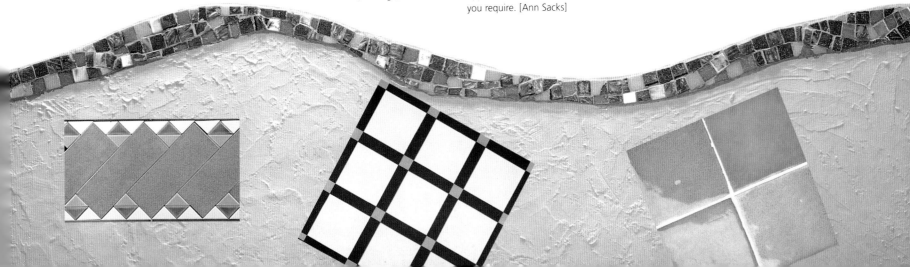

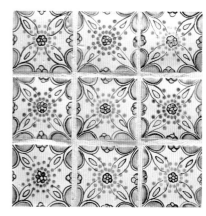

Moroccan quarry floor tiles

Four tiles form a medallion design in rich greens and blues on a cream ground. They would look good with a geometric-patterned border. [Country Floors]

Portuguese hand-painted wall tiles

Four tiles are used to form a decorative geometric motif, reminiscent of an heraldic design. They can be repeated across an entire wall area, or used to form drop-in panels. [Country Floors]

Hand-decorated glazed wall tiles

This panel of patterned tiles could be set into a border of plain green tiles and grouted in white. Alternatively, they could be used to form a border around plain tiles for a less busy look. [Corres Mexican Tiles]

Glazed wall and floor tiles

These tiles have a matte-glaze and can be used to make up a mosaic panel. The blue and light green central tiles are offset by a muted olive surround. [Country Floors]

Moroccan handmade encaustic floor tiles

These are made from powdered stone, marble and cement, then cured and dried. Tan and pale ocher plain tiles can be set inside this decorative double border to suggest a Moroccan hand-crafted rug. [Carreaux de Casbah]

Moroccan handmade encaustic floor tiles

Green and ocher field tiles are set diamond-fashion inside a vine-leaf trail border. A simple outer border of ocher tiles finishes the effect. [Carreaux de Casbah]

The green color of nature lends itself to "natural" designs. All of these are based on leaves and flowers but are given a geometric flavor in their execution. [l to r: Société Carré (a), Rye Tiles (b), Country Floors (c), Carreaux de Casbah (d, e), Ann Sacks (f)]

Mexican glazed wall tiles

Floral and plain tiles in various shades of green are shown. Experiment in this way to decide which color in the floral design to emphasize with coordinating field tiles. [Corres Mexican Tiles]

Mexican hand-painted glazed wall tiles

The bright geometric patterns in two colors on a warm cream background form a bold design. The tile surface is characteristically uneven. [Elon Tiles]

Glazed ceramic wall tiles

This selection of tiles features glossy relief patterns and intricate geometric and botanical pictorial features. They would be ideal for a conservatory or around a large, Victorian-style fireplace. [Shelly]

Portuguese hand-painted glazed wall tiles

This four-tile panel builds up to create a classic geometric Gothic pattern. It can be set into a plain wall area, or used to build up a stunning overall effect. [Country Floors]

Glazed wall tiles

These tiles have a beautiful flowing design and a border stripe. They are suitable as a border to plain tiles on splashbacks and are particularly good for fireplaces. [Shelly]

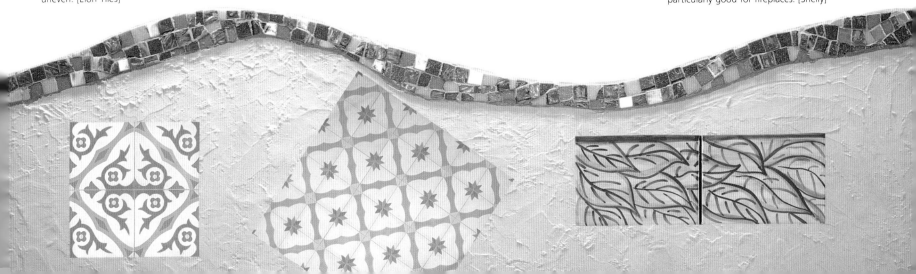

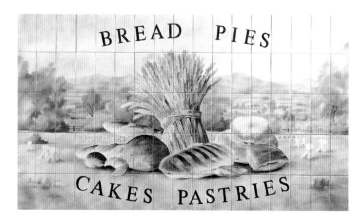

Hand-decorated wall panel

This panel is built up using oblong tiles, their length helping to accentuate the distance in the country scene. They can be framed with border tiles, a plain frieze, or a molded border. The panel would be suitable for a bakery or a kitchen without a view. [Sally Anderson Ceramics]

American hand-painted glazed wall tiles

These tiles are used to build up an Oriental theme to create an unusual and exotic panel. Ideal for Oriental-themed dining rooms, bathrooms or even a restaurant. [Hastings]

Hand-painted, hand-glazed wall tiles

This nine-tile panel creates a country scene. One panel could be used in a small kitchen but four would "balance" a larger room. They are suitable for splashbacks behind burners (hobs) and ranges or above a sink on a windowless wall. [Country Tile Design]

Welsh glazed wall tiles

A narrow mosaic painted border frames the picture of the fruit tree design to produce a beautiful mural. [Chantecler Ceramics]

Hand-painted glazed wall tiles

The hand-dragged border and harlequin tile pattern in greens and blues is combined with a fruit bowl motif to add visual interest to wall areas. [Decorum Ceramic Studio]

The emphasis here is on the fruits of nature – fruits, berries, plants, fish and waterfowl all look wonderful when using the color green as the design theme. [*l to r:* Tiles of Stow *(a)*, Jones's Tiles *(b)*, Ann Sacks *(c, e, f, g, h)*, Shelly *(d)*]

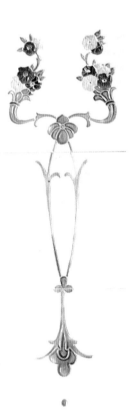

Hand-painted, embossed glazed tiles

Three tiles build up to form a combination panel which can be used for dados; to drop into a panel of plain field tiles for walls; or as an inset in a traditional fireplace. The tear-drop design is reminiscent of Art Nouveau. [Acquisitions]

Italian hand-decorated glazed clay wall tiles

These tiles have an Art Nouveau pattern and are combined with ridged and patterned border tiles at the base and a patterned border at the top to form a slim decorative panel for bathroom walls. [Hastings]

American hand-crafted clay wall tiles

These textured glazed tiles depict a dragonfly, spider and web, butterfly, gecko, salamander and frog on sea greens and blue bases. They could be used as borders and drop-ins to create panels. [Ann Sacks]

American hand-painted glazed wall tiles

The luscious fruits and vegetables have rich green leaves and green glaze outline. They can be used as border tiles, drop-ins or to create exciting wall panels – ideal in a restaurant or speciality food store! [Country Floors]

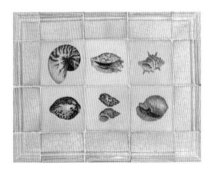

Handmade, hand-painted crackle-glazed Continental wall tiles

Crackle-glazed tiles and relief border and corner tiles are combined with molded seashell relief tiles in a range of subtle greens. Use them for kitchen splashbacks and countertops, shower enclosures, bathroom panels, etc. [Paris Ceramics]

Hand-decorated glazed wall tiles

The seaside motifs are in clear colors on an antique white ground. They have a light, "fresh" appeal. [Tiles of Stow]

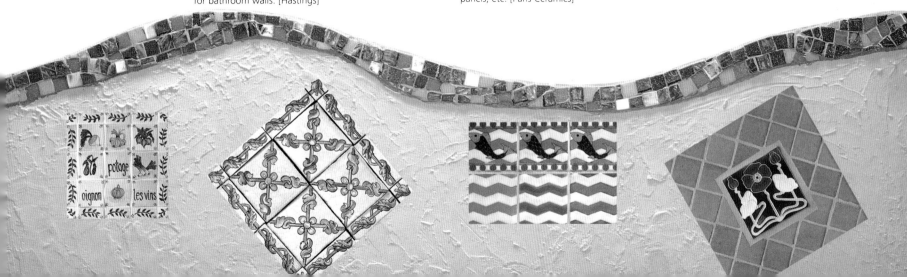

American hand-crafted terra clay tiles
A rustic Irish thistle border surrounds mottled green field tiles. These are suitable for floors and countertops and are also frostproof so could be used in a patio area. [Ann Sacks]

Hand-crafted mosaic field and border tiles
These tiles can be used for interior walls in conservatories, halls, kitchens, bathrooms, etc., and exterior walls (frostproof) for pools, patios, roof terraces, fountain splashbacks. The ribbons on the border tiles have a silver luster finish which produces a weathered patina, ideal for outdoor settings. [Ann Sacks]

Natural stone mosaic border and field tiles
Here, a lotus mosaic border is used to outline diamond-set antiqued stone slabs, ideal for countertops, floors, walls, conservatories and pool side. [Ann Sacks]

Natural antiqued stone
These tiles are set in typical tesselated style to form a panel which could be a centerpiece for a floor or wall area, or form a classical repeating pattern. [Ann Sacks]

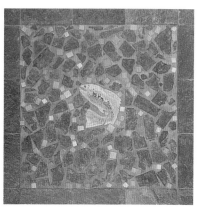

Hand-crafted mosaics
This jumping fish mosaic, set into a sea-green border panel, can be used in conservatories, around pools or for patios. [Ann Sacks]

Mosaics have been appreciated since ancient times and have an undeniable elegance. They look good in "watery" settings and raised relief borders frame them perfectly. [l to r: Ann Sacks (a, c, h, i), Hastings (b), Shelly (d, f), Country Floors (e, g)]

American luster-glazed wall tiles
Combined with a molded border tile and topped with a narrow nosing, these tiles create a classically simple, elegant treatment for kitchens, bathrooms and utility area – even hall dados. [Country Floors]

Terracotta floor tile and embossed border
The embossed vine border and square corners outline the plain terracotta tile to form a distinctive classical look. [Country Floors]

Relief-decorated frieze
The bear, fruit and branch motif is offset by plain glazed tiles and would be ideal to create a traditional tiled dado. [Country Floors]

Glazed ceramic wall tiles
Mix and match tile shapes to create an endless variety of patterned borders. The relief liners are used individually rather than joined up for a more unusual look. [Shelly]

American handmade glazed terracotta wall tiles
A leafy hand-painted border is added to plain glazed field tiles, showing how interesting effects can be built up using plain, patterned and molded tiles – all it takes is a little imagination! [Hastings]

Glazed terracotta tiles
The theme here is Celtic. A raised relief lion and stag are surrounded with small square mosaics and edged with Celtic knotwork. Larger panels could be built up and used to create stunning features for a conservatory. [Ann Sacks]

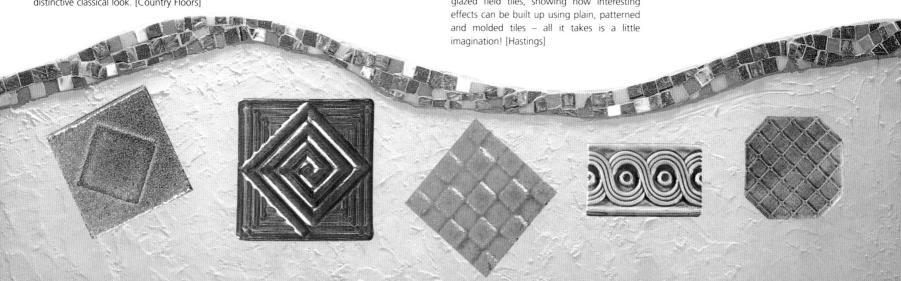

MOODY
BLUES

BLUE IS THE COLOR OF PEACE AND HARMONY. IT CAN BE
USED TO CREATE A CALM, RESTFUL AMBIENCE AND
TO BALANCE AN OVER-BRIGHT ROOM. BLUE
ALSO HAS A SPACE-MAKING QUALITY
WHICH CAN ENLARGE A SMALL
ROOM VISUALLY, ALTHOUGH
THE DEEPER TONES ARE
MORE ENCLOSING. ITS
COMPLEMENTARY
COLOR IS
ORANGE.

BLUE
TILE
DIRECTORY

*B*lue is the color of peace and harmony. It is also associated with chivalry, romance, devotion and loyalty. In heraldry it symbolizes piety and sincerity; in mythology it is the color of the sky gods Jupiter, Juno and Mercury. The rich blues seen in paintings and illuminated manuscripts from the Middle Ages were made using a precious natural pigment and reserved for the Virgin Mary's mantle, often enhanced with gold.

Blue can create a calm, restful ambience and is reputed to lower blood pressure, the pulse rate and brain waves; it can be particularly effective when used in the paler values in hospitals or schools. The deeper tones of blue suggest the velvety richness of a night sky or the infinite depth of the ocean, and seem more enclosing. Most blues (especially the blue-greens) can be chilly or even icy unless they are combined with some of the warmer tones in the spectrum − for instance, terracotta, apricot or burnt orange (the complementary color of blue).

Blue is a cool, receding color and has a space-making quality which helps to enlarge small rooms visually. Blue also has a fairly low reflectance value so it will diffuse and soften strong light − for instance, the paler values of blue will calm an over-bright or very sunny room. The bolder shades can be strident, so it may be best to confine them to accents and accessories, or use them to add depth and contrast to a pale scheme. Specific blues can be used to create a particular

period flavor. Delft and Wedgwood blues, in the seventeenth and eighteenth centuries respectively, were teamed with rich woods, pewter and silver, contrasted with white, and offset with warm-colored fabrics — a look easy to copy today for a stylish, traditional setting. Blue and white is also associated with the oriental style (the Willow Pattern), which can be replicated by mixing with pale woods, bamboo and lacquer reds. Paler, faded blues used with creamy white, yellow, gold and distressed paintwork and/or furniture suggest a slightly shabby chic Swedish Gustavian theme. A particular shade of gray-blue is synonymous with Shaker style on tiles, floors, woodwork and furniture.

Wall tiles in a strong turquoise, blue-green or sky-blue contrasted with terracotta floor carrés and touches of ocher and sunny yellow suggest the Mediterranean style and add dramatic impact to a hallway or dining room. A kitchen, too, could benefit from this treatment.

Misty and lilac-blues are colors of romance and work well in bedrooms and bathrooms teamed with soft sweet-pea colors. Alternatively, use these blues to decorate a small, sunless room, combined with touches of deep golden yellow, to create a calm, "studious" ambience in a study or home office.

Cleanliness and freshness are synonymous with blue — e.g. the color of swimming-pool tiles. Blue combined with green creates an even fresher feel — but there must be enough tonal contrasts in the scheme to make it work.

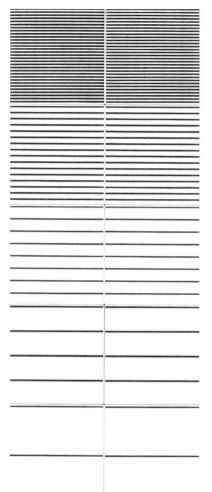

Natural textured quarried slate
The deep blue-gray offsets the complementary burnt orange, set diamond-fashion. Use for floors, inside and out, and seal with special slate sealant. [Ann Sacks]

Hand-painted glazed clay wall tiles
Build up a bold, strong overall design in geometric patterns – use carefully in small spaces or where the tiles need to be cut awkwardly, as this could be visually disturbing. [Country Floors]

Italian glazed wall tiles
In plain, richly colored glazes and coordinating graphic linear pattern, these tiles can be combined to suggest a modern minimalist theme. [Hastings]

Glass mosaics
These mosaic tiles will make a beautiful wall or floor decoration. The various values of blue can be combined to create very different and subtle effects. [Hastings]

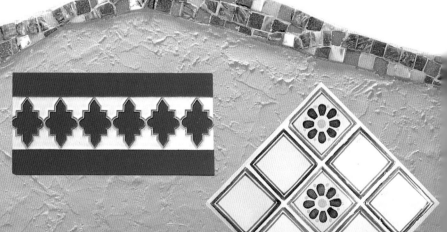

Although blue is a cool color, the range of tones available – from palest blue, through turquoise, to lilac blues, cobalt and dark navy – can produce amazingly different effects [l to r: Ann Sacks (a, b, f), Elon Tiles (c), Hastings (d), Corres Mexican Tiles (e), Shelly (g)]

Hand-crafted molded tiles
The central poppy tile will produce an original effect on walls, fireplaces, etc. It is set in a simulated mosaic styling of blue-gray field tiles, laid diamond-fashion. [Ann Sacks]

Italian hand-decorated glazed wall tiles
These tiles form a bold geometric pattern. This type of pattern can be grouted in a strong color to link with one of the colors in the tiles for extra definition. [Ideal Times]

Italian matte-glazed clay tiles
These tiles can be used to form a distinctive checkerboard pattern with plain coordinating field tiles, or as borders or panels. [Hastings]

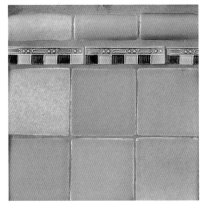

Molded glazed border and field tiles
The Georgian molded liner is set above blue-and-white checkerboard field tiles for dado areas, splashbacks, etc. [Ann Sacks]

Machine-made gloss-glazed wall tiles
The blues in different tones have been arranged to add pattern interest to plain blank walls. Mixed blues create a cool color scheme for a fresh effect in bathrooms and poolside. [H & R Johnson]

Hand-crafted molded tiles
A mini-geometric design border is combined with round nosing and gloss-glazed field tiles in blue-green. The jewel-bright colors in the border enliven the overall effect. [Ann Sacks]

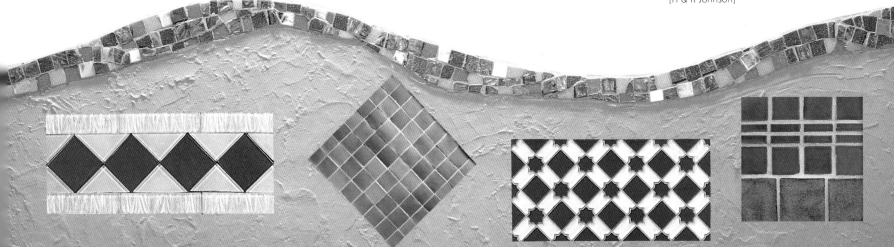

Islamic quarry tiles
Four tiles combine to form a workable module which can be repeated across a surface or used as drop-in panels for floors, walls, fireplaces and countertops. The motifs set a Gothic theme. [Ann Sacks]

Hand-crafted molded rustic tiles
The scarabs, snails and other animals have a mosaic styling and are used as drop-ins. Use on floors (light use), countertops, fireplaces, hearths, walls, exteriors, etc. [Ann Sacks]

Glazed quarry tiles
The rich orangey-red patterned border enlivens the matte-glazed plain field tiles. The beading has a subtle metallic luster to give an antiqued effect. [Ann Sacks]

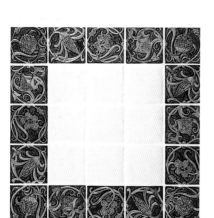

Hand-painted glazed wall tiles
The spiraling Persian border in soft pinks and greens on a strong blue ground is typical of William de Morgan's Arts & Crafts color combinations. [Winchester Tile Company]

Glazed ceramic tiles
The bright orange and green patterned tiles are coordinated with a deep blue strip border and make an attractive kitchen panel when set amongst matching solid blue field tiles. The corner tiles from the border are used to form the central motif. [Corres Mexican Tiles]

Majolica-glazed European terracotta tiles
The off-white crackle-glaze, together with the yellow and pink flowers, warms up the cooler blues in the design. [Country Floors]

Glazed quarry tiles
Plain tiles are combined with decorative and molded borders – as these have a distinct Arts & Crafts/Edwardian flavor, they are particularly suitable for hall dados in houses of the period. [Ann Sacks]

Many of the most well-known tile designs – such as Delft – are in blue. Blue tiles on a white background have a clean, classic elegance which is hard to match. [*l to r:* Hastings (*a, f, g*), Ann Sacks (*b, c, d*), Corres Mexican Tiles (*e*)]

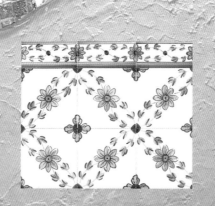

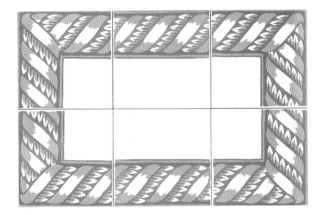

Hand-printed floor and wall tiles
Create a bold border effect with these tiles to enhance a traditional theme. They are strong blue and soft green on pale bone-colored glaze and can be laid in many combinations. [Rye Tiles]

Spanish glazed clay tiles
These tiles are wood-fired to a traditional European method used for over 2000 years. A blue braided border surrounds crackle-glazed field tiles, set diamond-fashion. They are suitable for walls, countertops and floors. [Ann Sacks]

Stoneware mosaics
These come on an easy-to-handle flexible mesh backing. The soft blue and cream flowing lotus border is used to outline square-set antiqued stone slabs. Use them for countertops, floors, walls, conservatories, pool sides, as panel insets in walls and floors – or use the border mosaics to trim walls and floors. [Ann Sacks]

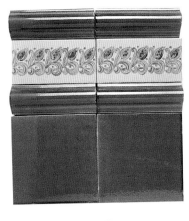

Majolica-glazed terracotta tiles
These tiles can be used to create panels, frames or to outline features on floors (light use; not outside in cold countries) and walls. The deep blue leaf border is softened by the juxtaposition of turquoise. [Country Floors]

Glazed ceramic wall tiles
An interesting effect is created by combining a marble patterned border with highly glossed nosing on either side. [Corres Mexican Tiles]

Portuguese hand-painted wall plaque
Use this classic blue and white border to frame house names and numbers or company names which can either be painted on tiles or some other surface. Try hand-painting or stenciling your own! [Countr Floors]

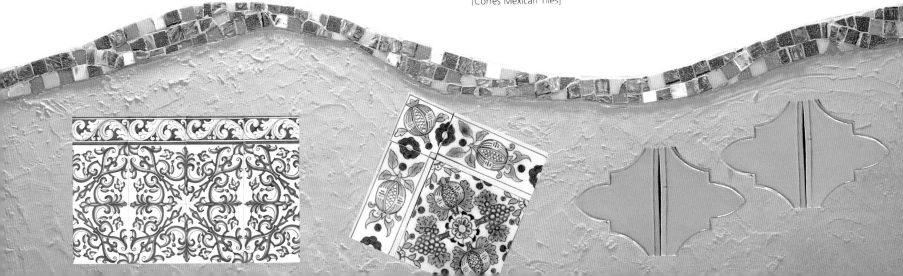

Mexican glazed wall tiles
This pretty panel features two bluebirds and a butterfly amongst blue and orange flowers and olive green leaves. The border acts as a picture frame. [Corres Mexican Tiles]

American hand-decorated faience-glazed terracotta tiles
In classic blue and white, these wall tiles can be used to create an overall pattern or as a distinctive border. [Country Floors]

Spanish glazed clay wall tiles
Combined with a decorative border in blues and greens, incorporating copper glaze for extra shine, these tiles will create a Gothic effect. Use on walls or fireplaces for authentic architectural detail. [Country Floors]

Machine-made, screen-printed glazed tiles
Use these tiles as a splashback or feature panel as is, or adjusted to create a border/frieze effect. [Caroline & Stephen Atkinson-Jones]

Molded glazed wall tiles
The jewel-bright sapphire blue is stunning. "Ribbon" effect tiles are combined with a molded rope border and liners, and could be used as a dado trim on a wall of plain or patterned tiles. [Shelly]

Hand-decorated ceramic tiles
Use these tiles as drop-in panels or in a larger grouping to create a bold geometric effect. [Country Floors]

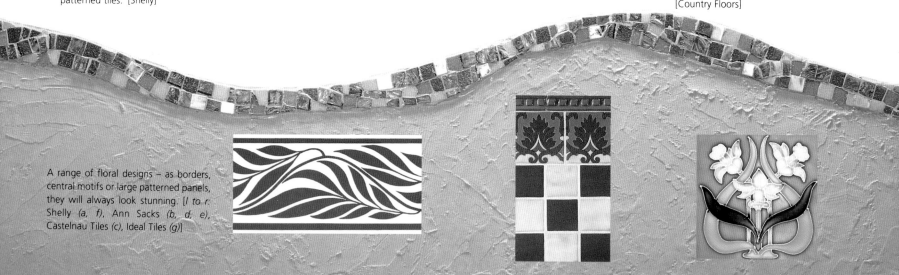

A range of floral designs – as borders, central motifs or large patterned panels, they will always look stunning. [l to r: Shelly (a, f), Ann Sacks (b, d, e), Castelnau Tiles (c), Ideal Tiles (g)]

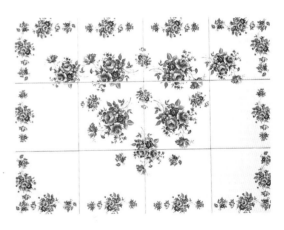

Screen-printed glazed tiles
This decorative 12-tile panel of blue posies on a white ground was inspired by a Victorian botanical etching. There are endless design possibilities for kitchens, bathrooms, utility areas, showers, etc. [Caroline & Stephen Atkinson-Jones]

Portuguese hand-decorated glazed ceramic wall tiles
Four tiles build up to form a decorative panel which can be used as a drop-in or on a wall of plain tiles, or to create an overall effect – this four-tile module could be hung across a wall to form a distinct trellis pattern. [Ideal Tiles]

Glazed wall tiles
This relief tile in sapphire blue would look perfect as an occasional drop-in tile on a plain wall or to create a textured border. [Shelly]

Handmade glaze-fired wall tiles
Nine tiles build up into a bouquet of white daisies in a terracotta pot on a deep cobalt blue ground. Match coordinating tiles with a single central motif. [Chantecler Ceramics]

Hand-crafted glazed tiles
Swimming fish, set into a mosaic background, can be combined with blue grout for a realistic sea theme. [Ann Sacks]

Glazed wall tiles
These tiles are designed to be used as a border or frieze and are painted with reproductions of original Arts & Crafts tiles designed by William de Morgan in the 19th century. This colorful fish frieze has fish swimming in a blue river with the swirling leaves forming part of the pattern. [Winchester Tile Company]

Hand-decorated glazed tiles
Build up an appealing ginger and white cat on a blue and white checkerboard floor, surrounded with 12 plain coordinating glazed tiles to form a frame. Use it as an eye-catching feature on a blank wall. [Shelly]

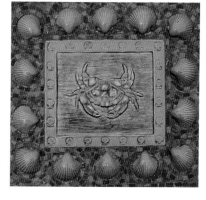

Spanish glazed clay tiles
Blue fish "swim" across the tiles and are combined with a simple striped border and shell corners. A blue grout would define the pattern more clearly. [Ann Sacks]

American hand-crafted glazed relief tiles
Combine these tiles with flat ones, in stoneware or terracotta for floors and walls, both inside and out (stoneware is frostproof) – for poolside, conservatory or where a shellfish image is appropriate. [Ann Sacks]

Hand-painted wall panel
These are a few of the many nautical-themed tiles available. Patterns can be made up for walls, light flooring, countertops, fireplaces, etc. [Ann Sacks]

These tiles show a wide range of pictorial motifs which are available in blue, from sea-themed designs to country houses. [l to r: Decorum Ceramic Studio (a), Country Floors (b, g), Napiorkowska (c), Ann Sacks (d), Ideal Tiles (e), Tiles of Stow (f)]

Hand-decorated, glazed wall tiles
These fruit and vegetable motifs can be used, combined with matching border tiles, to build up a mural; as a random pattern; to create a patchwork effect; or as drop-ins in a wall of plain field tiles. [Shelly]

Brazilian handmade, hand-decorated glazed tiles
These Delft-style tiles are made from wet clay using a 17th-century Dutch technique. They have an authentic look and can be used around fireplaces, stoves and in kitchens and dairies. [Fired Earth]

Hand-painted border and picture tiles
The whimsical sun and moon design in complementary warm yellow and orange is set against a brilliant blue background. Here, they are set as a panel which could decorate interior walls in household and commercial situations. [Decorum Ceramic Studio]

American faience-glazed terracotta wall tiles
A panel is built up from nine tiles to form mythological sun and moon faces with a decorative circular border. Set it into a wall of blue and white field tiles. [Country Floors]

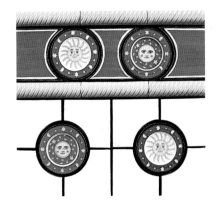

Glazed wall tiles
These tiles are combined with molded border tiles and nosings. The blue and yellow combination sets a sunny scene. [Shelly]

NEUTRALS
AND
NATURALS

TRUE NEUTRALS ARE PURE WHITE, BLACK AND GRAY.
ACCEPTED NEUTRALS ARE COLORS ASSOCIATED
WITH NATURAL MATERIALS AND FIBERS, AND
"TINTED" WHITES. THESE COLORS ARE
SOFTER AND EASIER TO USE THAN
BLACK AND WHITE, AND CAN
ENHANCE A SCHEME BY
OFFSETTING RICH, WARM
COLORS. THEY CAN
ALSO BE USED
ON THEIR
OWN.

NEUTRAL AND NATURAL
TILE DIRECTORY

Neutral and natural colors are, strictly speaking, not colors at all – that is, they are not made by mixing hues together and do not appear on the color wheel. In interior design, neutral and natural colors usually provide a link in, or the definition to, a color scheme, but can also be used on their own. Neutrals often form the background to a patterned fabric, flooring or wallcovering, or are used for a "field" tile.

Neutrals can be divided into two groups: true and accepted neutrals. True neutrals are pure white, black and various values of pure gray, made by mixing black and white together in varying proportions to achieve different tones. Used alone, white and gray can be cold, stark and uninviting, and black tends to be somber as it absorbs light, so it needs to be combined with an interesting surface texture. Black, white and gray are discussed in a separate section.

Accepted neutrals are the colors associated with natural materials and fibers – for instance, jute, burlap (hessian), flax, seagrass, sisal, rush matting, natural stone and wood. They include beiges, creams, off-whites, fawns, taupes, mushroom, magnolia and soft browns, and are all easy on the

eye and comfortable to live with. However, they can also be bland and safe if they are not enlivened with some bold accents and strong textural contrasts.

"Tinted" whites are also accepted neutrals and are found in most paint ranges, as field tiles and as the background to colored patterns. All the accepted neutrals relate to the original hues in the spectrum and are very pale values of the pure color made with the addition of white. For instance, there are peach and pinkish beiges, yellow creams, bluish off-whites, gray-greens and blue-grays. All these neutrals need very careful color-matching.

The colors of natural materials and fibers are much softer and easier to use than black, white or gray. They can contribute a slightly weathered or aged look to a scheme, or suggest a subtle "shabby chic" ambience. Select neutrals to enhance the theme – creamy or yellowish neutrals to offset rich, warm color schemes (chestnut brown, Indian reds, terracotta, gold and ocher) and cooler beiges and "greiges" with the bolder blues and greens.

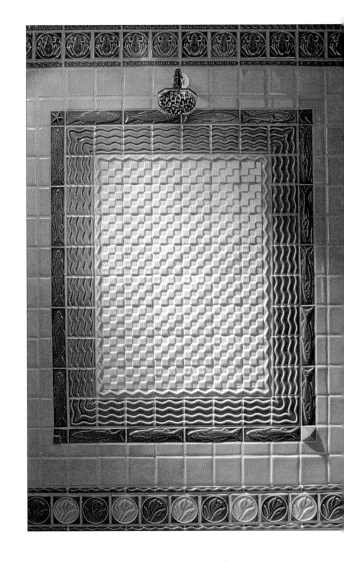

These colors can also be used on their own to create a relaxing scheme. However, it is important to choose from the same color palette to avoid a disturbing clash and to vary the tones. It is essential to achieve a really good textural contrast with shiny, rustic, silky, matte, rough, shaggy and sheer light-filtering surfaces.

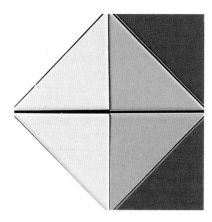

Italian matte-glazed clay tiles
In a choice of solid colors – black, grays, whites and neutrals – these tiles are cut in a triangular shape and set to form a diamond trellis effect. They can be used for floors, walls and fireplaces. [Hastings]

Natural riven slate tiles
Multicolored slate has a natural veining and can be installed either side up to allow emphasis of the attractive natural shading. They can be used for floors inside and out, as they are slip-resistant in wet areas and thus good for shower rooms and poolside. [Ann Sacks]

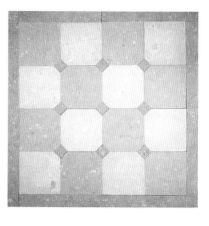

Italian quarried limestone flagstones
With natural fossils embedded in the stone, these tiles give a timeless, traditional feel. For residential floors, they must be sealed with a penetrating non-slip sealer. [Ann Sacks]

Unglazed vitrified floor tiles
These 19th-century-style floor tiles are used to recreate an Edwardian style floor, ideal for restoration work or in period buildings for halls, verandas, porches, etc. [H & R Johnson]

Unglazed terracotta floor tiles
These tiles can be laid in a variety of ways to create traditional effects and combined with borders to outline features or to define the shape of the room. [Marston & Langinger]

Neutrals and naturals work perfectly with every color in the spectrum. They can be used in simple geometric designs or with detailed patterns – either way, they will never appear overdominating. [l to r: Hastings (a), Shelly (b), Winchester Tile Company (c), Country Floors (d), H & R Johnson (e)]

Natural floor tiles

The pale cream border tiles are ideal for emphasizing the richly colored insets. The range of natural materials is enormous and the different types can be laid together, as here, or used to create a tonal color scheme. [Country Floors]

Natural slate floor tiles

Rows of natural-colored diamonds are coordinated with square orange and red tiles which are simply stronger shades of the diamonds. [Country Floors]

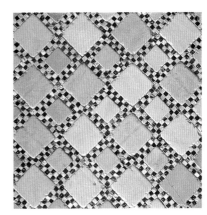

Italian mosaics and antiqued stone

Laid in diamond checkerboard fashion, these tiles create a look of timeless elegance for walls, floors, countertops, hearths, etc. This type of treatment will increase the apparent width and size of narrow corridors and small floor areas. [Ann Sacks]

Unglazed vitrified floor tiles

These 19th-century tiles are combined with geometric cut tiles from a range of neutral and deep rich colors. Here, they are used to create the look of an authentic Victorian encaustic floor. [H & R Johnson]

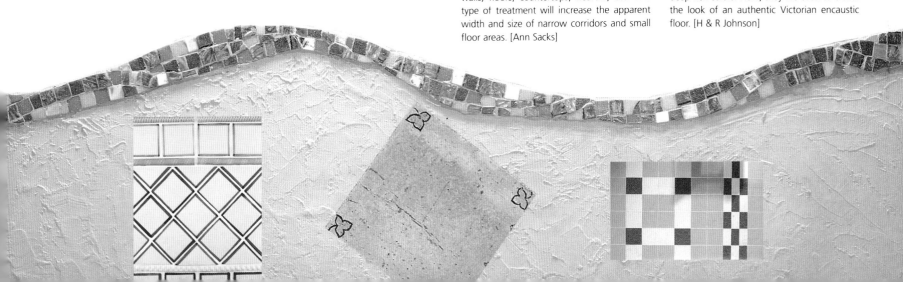

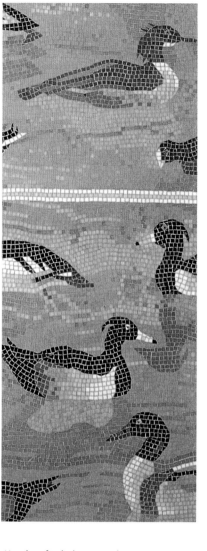

Hand-decorated glazed tiles
A Delft-inspired figurative tile is set into a panel of neutral ceramic field tiles which can be used to make a feature of a large, open wall. [Elon]

English hand-decorated glazed tiles
Four tiles are used to form a mural depicting a friendly cow in a harvest field. Mural panels can be used to drop into a wall of field tiles, or as an integral part of a splashback or behind a stove. [Country Floors]

Hand-decorated glazed clay wall tiles
This East wind motif border pattern can be used to trim the top of a plain wall, or individually as drop-ins with a ceramic soap dish decorated to match. [Country Floors]

Hand-painted glazed tile
A vividly colored fish painted onto a glazed tile is set into tumbled botticino marble to add color interest to a natural creamy wall or floor surface. [Country Floors]

Hand-crafted glass mosaics
Waterfowl – geese, ducks, drakes and gulls – are depicted on a mosaic wall panel. Mosaics can be used to create a *trompe l'oeil* effect for pools and fountains. [Mosaic Workshop]

American hand-decorated glazed porcelain wall tile
This tile depicts an array of seashells. It can be used to form a border, a definite pattern or as random drop-ins. [Country Floors]

Neutral and natural tiles are often teamed with fruit and flower designs though they work equally well with other pictorial motifs, particularly those in traditional style. [l to r: Elon (a, b), Ann Sacks (c, g), Country Floors (d, e, f)]

Natural stone tiles

The mood here is ancient Greece and Rome, with figurative scenes drawn to give a *trompe l'oeil* effect, echoing classical sculpture. [Country Floors]

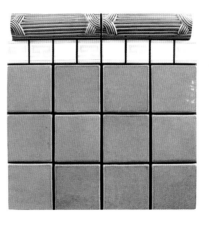

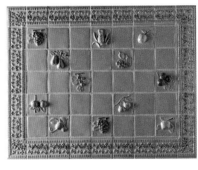

Traditional slate tiles

These pewter-gray tiles produce a clean, minimalist look. The ridged nosing and Greek-key border add a touch of decoration to what may otherwise be too cold a look. [Shelly]

Handmade raised-pattern wall tiles

The different fruit patterns stand out in relief against a high-glaze off-white background. Here, the tiles are set into a panel, interspersed with a plain glazed off-white base tile and framed with coordinating border and corner tiles. [Corres Mexican Tiles]

Glazed ceramic wall tiles

White tiles are given a touch of warmth and sparkle with a combination of neutral and brightly colored diamond insets. The fruit border sets a Bacchanalian theme. [Shelly]

Polished marble tiles

Trompe l'oeil pictures of fruit are set into square marble tiles and topped with a fruit border. [Country Floors]

Clay wall tiles

This range of plain, textured relief and patterned tiles would look good in any room. The brown and cream tones work very well with ethnic designs and earth colors. [Shelly]

Textured glazed wall tiles

These tiles have a classic, timeless look. It is possible to build up wall features, panels, dados, alcoves, frames and architraves from a range of heavy relief, neutral-colored tiles. [Ann Sacks]

Hand-cut stone and marble mosaics
These mosaics are set into a classical Greek-key border design to give architectural definition to a grand hall, dining and living room, or conservatory floors. [Paris Ceramics]

Natural stone and marble mosaics
Mosaics afford wonderful creative design possiblities. Terracotta, soft pink, white, gray and black mosaics are used to form a classical pattern of rope and Greek-key borders for walls and floors. [Shelly]

Traditional marble mosaics
Natural/neutral colors can be combined to create a typical Romanesque effect for walls and floors in older-style properties or for swimming pools, conservatories, patios and garden rooms. [Hastings]

Antiqued stone with limestone and quarried slate
Random-size small travertino stones are combined with bar liners to create borders, frames and patterns. [Ann Sacks]

"Biblical" stone tiles (over 500 years old from Israel)
Here, Roman stone is set with a Roman border in classical chain-link pattern. Use these tiles for floors and walls, both inside and out, where a characteristic traditional textured look is required and grout in a pale color for maximum effect. [Ann Sacks]

Antique stone with limestone and quarried slate
Small stones are set brick-pattern and combined with relief and slim rail liners for a subtle yet sophisticated effect. [Ann Sacks]

Antiqued stone with limestone and quarried slate
Creamy travertino stones are combined with limestone and quarried gray slate to suggest a *trompe l'oeil* border for a traditional classical treatment. [Ann Sacks]

Small scale tiles and mosaics in neutral colors are combined with earth tones and jewel-bright splashes for maximum effect. The plain colors and square shapes are contrasted with star bursts, triangles and octagons to play visual geometric "tricks." [l to r: Hastings (a, c), Country Floors (b, d, e), Ann Sacks (f)]

 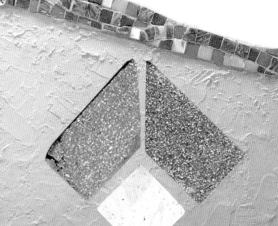

Hand-crafted molded glazed tiles
Set in a diamond fashion, these tiles provide a unifying design concept for internal walls, countertops, splashbacks, showers, fireplaces, etc. Some of the tiles have crackle glazes, which are not suitable for very wet situations or countertops. [Ann Sacks]

Antiqued stone with limestone and quarried slate
The natural colors of limestone contain warm pinkish tones, which is offset with a slate-gray triangular geometric border, topped with a bullnose bar liner. [Ann Sacks]

Natural marble and limestone tiles
Square creamy white tiles have small beige-gray diamond insets to provide pattern interest and are bordered with random-cut limestone to create a softly flowing geometric design. [Shelly]

Natural stone tiles
In natural/neutral colors, these tiles form a random geometric pattern which is ideal for floors, walls and countertops. They can be sealed with beeswax for a rich patina. [Country Floors]

Aegean mosaics
This classical circular motif with a cream-colored leafy image makes maximum use of the natural beige and greenish tones of Aegean mosaics. [Ann Sacks]

Glazed ceramic wall tiles

Cool gray and white glazed tiles are cut to form triangles and narrow borders, offset by basic square tiles outlined with white grout. They are ideal for hot, steamy bathrooms and kitchens. [Elon]

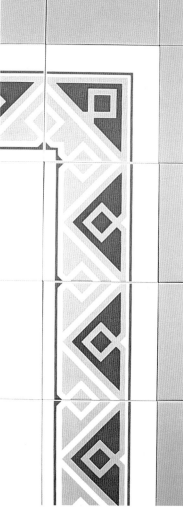

Italian marble floor tiles

Textured tiles are set as a squared panel for use in conservatories or around swimming pools – anywhere that a traditional rustic look will be in keeping with the decorating and architectural style. [Marston & Langinger]

Natural quarried slate

Riven slate does not have to be laid in traditional brick or edge-to-edge fashion. Here, green and olive slates are cut to create texture and pattern interest without being too bold in design terms. [Ann Sacks]

Antiqued stone and travertino

Warm beige stone tiles are laid brick pattern and defined by a braided mosaic liner in blue and terracotta at the top and a simple geometric strip below. [Ann Sacks]

Italian glazed floor and wall tiles

Creamy-neutral field tiles are trimmed with a hand-decorated border and corner tiles in crisp clear colors. Use them to create panels, or to border or outline features on floors and walls. [Hastings]

Natural quarried slate

Slate floor tiles in creamy gold and gray tones are unique as they are a natural quarried material. Triangles are framed with slim rail liners to create a formal pattern. [Ann Sacks]

Natural quarried slate

Calibrated natural slate has a slightly rough textured surface for safety (non-slip). Here, gray-green slate looks lighter with a pale gray grout. [Ann Sacks]

Borders, frames and checkerboard effects can be created using natural materials and neutral colors with tonal contrast. The effect will be more subtle and softer on the eye than similar patterns made with dark, bold or bright, contrasting colors. [l to r: Country Floors (a, c, d, e), Ann Sacks (b, f)]

Antiqued stone
Set on the slant, the intricate pattern of these tiles creates a feeling of depth. They are ideal where a monochromatic effect will offset a scheme in neutral colors. [Ann Sacks]

Antique terracotta blonde slabs
This reclaimed material is usually over 150 years old and will have wear layers on some slabs. Use them for floors and walls to achieve a Provencal style, and on patios and verandas in warm climates. [Ann Sacks]

Aegean mosaics and acid stone slabs
The stylized fish border swims around the central panel, but there are endless permutations combining these mosaic borders with slate, travertino and other stone slabs for individual decorative effect. Use them for walls, countertops, pools, etc. They are frostproof and skid resistant so they can be used outside and in commercial situations. [Ann Sacks]

Antiqued stone travertino slabs
These tiles create a classic, aged architectural effect and are trimmed with mosaic borders for extra color. Use for walls, floors, countertops, pools, showers, etc. They are ideal for outside use as they are frostproof. [Ann Sacks]

Antiqued stone
Mini-random pattern in light travertino looks like a mature sunwarmed stone wall, trimmed with a starburst border outlined in darker toffee-colored slabs. [Ann Sacks]

BLACK
AND
WHITE

BLACK ABSORBS LIGHT; WHITE GIVES MAXIMUM REFLECTION.
A MIDDLE-TONE GRAY WILL TAKE ON A LITTLE OF THE
COLOR IT LIES NEXT TO. BLACK AND WHITE CAN
BE DIFFICULT TO USE, BECOMING TOO OVER-
POWERING OR TOO GLARING, BUT WHEN
USED CAREFULLY, PARTICULARLY
WITH SHADES OF GRAY, THEY
CAN CREATE AN
UNSURPASSED
CLASSICAL
ELEGANCE.

BLACK AND WHITE
TILE
DIRECTORY

Black, white and gray are true neutrals (see NEUTRALS AND NATURALS). They do not appear on the color wheel. Gray is made by mixing black and white together in varying proportions to achieve different tones. Used alone, white and gray can be cold, stark and uninviting, and black tends to be somber as it absorbs light, so it needs to be combined with an interesting surface texture.

Black symbolizes darkness and death, and is the color of penitence, grief, mourning and sadness. It also has negative associations, such as Satan, witchcraft and black magic, and anarchy. However, black cats signify good luck in some cultures, and black clothes are seen as the epitomy of glamor, sophistication and elegance.

White is the natural complement to black, symbolizing as it does cleanliness, virginity, innocence and chastity. In heraldry the color white suggests faith and purity. To the Greeks and Hindus it was the color of pure water

and in ancient mythology it was associated with the moon goddess. However, a white elephant is a burdensome possession, and the white flag of truce is associated with surrender and disgrace. White is reputed to be the strongest light-reflecting surface there is, although in reality it can be clinical, harsh and stark – even grayish.

Gray is the color of wisdom and intelligence (e.g. gray matter, éminence grise) and bureaucracy.

It is also the color of insubstantial gossamer, cobwebs and shadows — and is therefore often associated with uniformity and self-effacing people who fade into the background. It is the color of drabness, urban landscape and city "concrete jungles." Pure, pale and middle-tone grays have a chameleon-like quality, taking on a little of the color with which they are used.

Used sparingly, black will sharpen up any color scheme, but when used excessively it can be overpowering. Black can dazzle or "strobe" — this usually happens with striped or check patterns when white or a strong color is used with black. White has maximum lightness and a shiny finish gives maximum reflection. White will often cool down a "hot" color scheme of reds, yellows or oranges, or add a special sparkle to dark, rich colors. Used with blue and a touch of sunny yellow, it creates a traditionally fresh kitchen or bathroom theme; combine it with black for timeless classical elegance. Use white on its own to create a sense of space.

Gray is much more user-friendly and versatile than black as it is less heavy and light-absorbing. Pale and middle-tone grays can be used to accent a dark or rich, warm scheme where white could be too glaring. Mix gray with soft pinks, lavenders, mauves and purples for a sophisticated, elegant scheme; or combine it with fondant pinks, aquamarine, lilac, lemon, coral, sky blue, peach and minty-greens for a more gentle effect. A scheme based on gray with black and white can be very flexible, appearing warm in winter and cool in summer if the right accents and accessories are used with them.

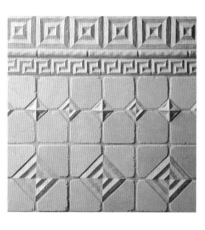

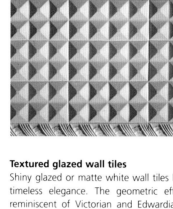

Molded glazed wall tiles

These tiles are frostproof and suitable for use on inside and outside walls. The patterns are varied, and many different effects can be created, all forming a classical and traditional European look. [Ann Sacks]

Matte-glazed wall tiles

This panel of Spanish-inspired tiles shows how an interesting dado and textured effect can be created with what is virtually a plain self-colored tile. Not all tiles have a shiny unwelcoming feel. [Ann Sacks]

Textured glazed wall tiles

Shiny glazed or matte white wall tiles have a timeless elegance. The geometric effect is reminiscent of Victorian and Edwardian hall dado design. [Ann Sacks]

American molded glazed liners

Depicting various neoclassical and traditional architectural themes – from rope, rose, shell, leaf and tassel to Greek key – these tiles can be combined with plain glazed tiles and corners to create panels, dados, etc. [Hastings]

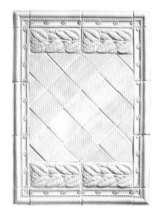

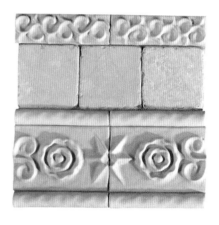

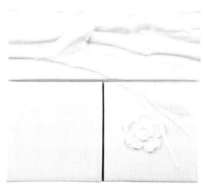

Plain and crackle-glazed wall tiles

Here, a warm white crackle-glazed plain-tile central panel is hung diamond-trellis fashion, and surrounded by a raised leaf border and small beaded border tiles as a concept design. [Ann Sacks]

Hand-crafted molded tiles

These simple raised border tiles have a stylized star and scroll design and have been molded to look like old plasterwork. [Ann Sacks]

American molded relief wall tiles

The use of a field tile, rose motif and antique white border tile featuring a molded branch will make a subtle wall decoration or splashback. [Country Floors]

This range of off-white tiles all have raised designs either on a single tile or as a border. The result is simple and subtle, yet extremely effective. [*l to r*: Country Floors *(a)*, Elon *(b, d, e)*, Hastings *(c)*]

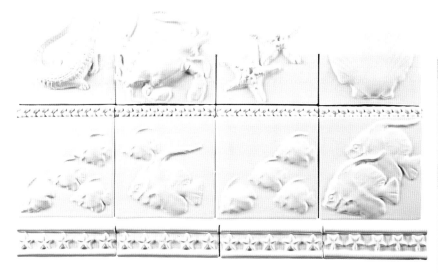

American molded and shaped glazed tiles
The sea theme motifs form a dado rail and are combined with classical molded liners in various depths to build up a highly original dado or panel. [Hastings]

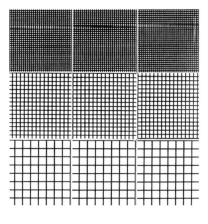

Screen-printed glazed wall tiles
This geometric, linear pattern is achieved by screen-printing and is ideal for a streamlined minimalist or hi-tech look in kitchens and bathrooms. [Hastings]

American molded glazed clay wall tiles
These tiles are in traditional "celestial" designs of moon, stars, sun and wind in soft antique white. Use them to create a border effect or to drop into a wall of plain glazed field tiles. [Country Floors]

Hand-crafted crackle-glazed wall tiles
These tiles are hung in a diamond pattern and interspersed with natural terracotta clay molded borders, with entwined acanthus and vine leaf or curling ribbon swags reminiscent of the 19th-century Arts & Crafts look. This combination can be used for indoor and exterior walls (a mild climate for the terracotta); the white tile is also suitable for some countertops. [Ann Sacks]

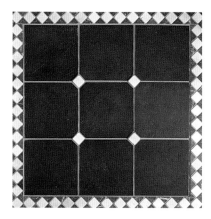

Quarried slate

These tiles are combined with a decorative diamond design border and white inserts to create an eye-catching geometric effect. Such combinations allow for many design possibilities. [Ann Sacks]

Luster-glazed clay tiles

This distinctive diamond design gives the effect of an optical illusion. Use such tiles carefully, particularly in a small room. [Shelly]

Hand-painted ceramic wall tiles

These plain black tiles have a range of abstract designs hand-painted in white. Use them as drop-ins in a bathroom to create a bold, modern Metropolitan look. [Ann Sacks]

Ceramic wall tiles

The white tile has an intricately painted black motif whilst the black tile has the same design as a raised relief which has been glazed to draw it forwards from its surround. [Shelly]

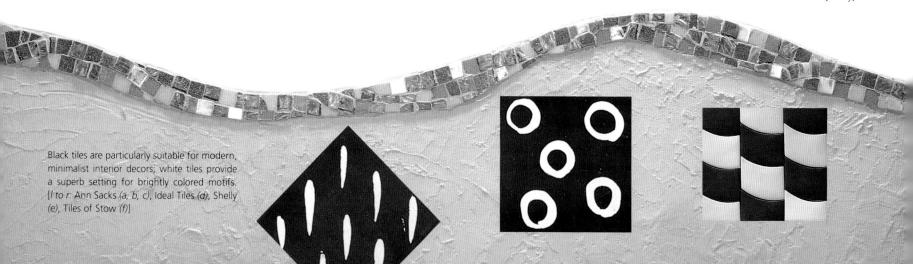

Black tiles are particularly suitable for modern, minimalist interior decors; white tiles provide a superb setting for brightly colored motifs. [*l to r:* Ann Sacks *(a, b, c)*, Ideal Tiles *(d)*, Shelly *(e)*, Tiles of Stow *(f)*]

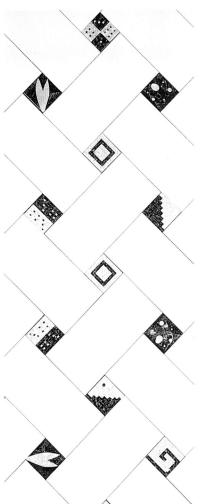

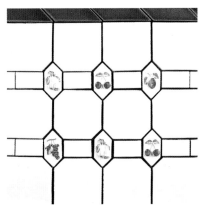

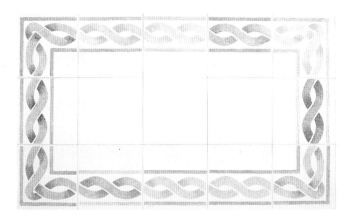

Glazed ceramic wall tiles
This panel suggesting stained glass would bring a cheerful ambience into a dark room. Use a colored grout to emphasize the design created by the various tile shapes. [Shelly]

Hand-decorated onglaze tiles
The onglaze technique combined with hand-painting creates an individual look. Here, the "rope" border stenciled design in soft colors on a white ground is combined with white field tiles to form a 15-tile panel, but other color combinations are possible. [Tiles of Stow]

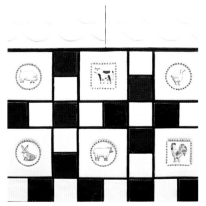

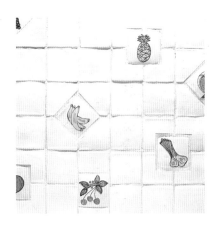

Italian glazed wall tiles
Oblong white tiles are laid trellis-fashion with decorated black and gray insets to produce a lively scatter pattern which would be ideal for a plain or dark area. [Hastings]

Glazed ceramic wall tiles
Black and white checkerboard tiles are interspersed with a bright array of "appliquéed" farm animals and topped with a raised "cloud" border. [Shelly]

Hand-painted glazed wall tiles
These tiles are decorated with motifs in clear colors on a white ground. Other designs such as fruits, leaves and flowers can be mixed and matched effectively with these culinary designs. [Ann Sacks]

Mexican hand-cut glazed wall tiles
Suitable for bathrooms, showers and kitchens, these tiles are combined with fruit designs. Here, variation is created by inserting some of the tiles diagonally. [Corres Mexican Tiles]

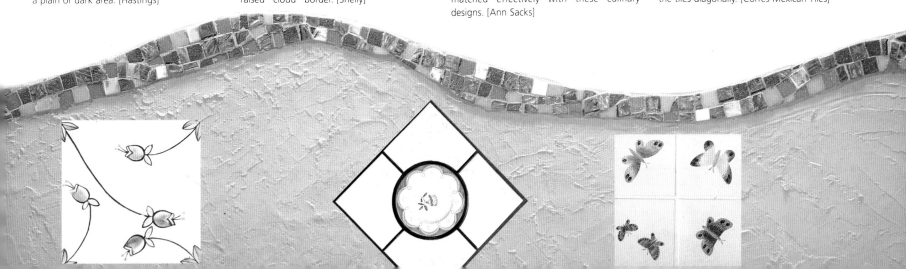

Handmade unglazed encaustic tiles
These stylized animal motif tiles create an attractive panel or border effect – they would be great fun on the floor, or as a changing-table top in a child's room. [Life Enhancing Tile Company]

American hand-molded glazed wall tiles
These tiles are used to create a concept panel with checkerboard border tiles, combined with plain field tiles, for walls and splashbacks. [Country Floors]

Clay wall and floor tiles
Black, blue-gray and off-white tiles are joined with lighter gray grout. The geometric star design would look good in a conservatory or large hall. [Country Floors]

Handmade unglazed encaustic tiles
Simple geometric patterns can be formed with combinations of these triangular tiles. They can be used on floors, walls, countertops (if sealed), fireplaces, splashbacks, etc. [Life Enhancing Tile Company]

Stone and glazed ceramic tiles
The matte stone provides a good visual foil to the rich green tiles. Combining different materials can produce interesting, attractive and often unusual results. [Country Floors]

Tumbled marble tiles
These tiles can be used to build up interesting geometric effects on both walls and floors. Use them to add cool Mediterranean character and style. [World's End Tiles]

Italian hand-painted wall tiles
Create a classical octagonal/inset look using a square module, topped with a slim diamond-patterned border for dados and splashbacks. [Country Floors]

"Be bold" is the order of the day here. 1920s motifs, geometric designs, dalmatian spots – all of these black-and-white designs could be a stand-out feature in any room. [l to r: Hastings (a, b, c, e), Country Floors (d), Mary Rose Young (f)]

Ceramic wall tiles
Black and prussian blue tiles are combined here with a white and gray background. The light-reflecting surface of the tiles would look good in a small bathroom. [Hastings]

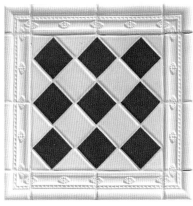

Spanish copper-glazed clay wall tiles
These tiles are laid in checkerboard pattern and topped with an egg-and-dart molded border in solid colors, and a chain-link decorated lower border. [Country Floors]

Matte-glazed clay wall tiles
Solid white and stone gray field tiles are laid diamond-fashion with a raised relief white border which has the effect of a picture frame. The central tile panel could be used on a wall or work surface. [Ann Sacks]

Glazed ceramic wall tiles
Stars and diamonds are given a sumptuous treatment by the addition of a thin gold inlay. The use of star insets rather than square ones gives an Islamic feel to this traditional trellis design. [Ann Sacks]

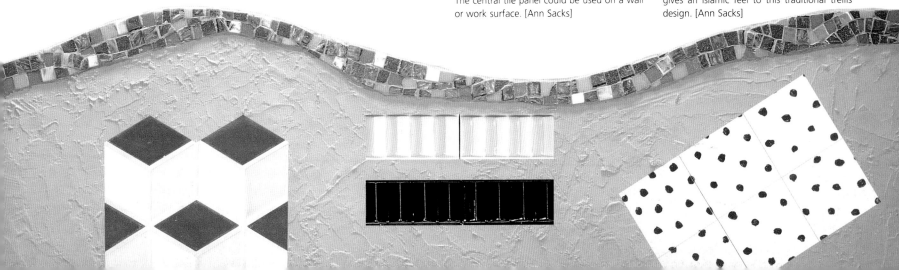

SHIMMERING
METALLICS

METALLICS USUALLY HAVE AN ATTRACTIVE GLEAM AND
A RICH SURFACE. GOLD, BRASS AND COPPER ARE
WARM; SILVER, PLATINUM AND PEWTER HAVE A
COOL QUALITY. A METALLIC SURFACE
INCREASES THE STRENGTH AND
EFFECT OF A COLORED TILE
AND CAN IMPROVE A
ROOM WITH RICH
OPULENCE OR COOL
SOPHISTICATION.

METALLIC

TILE
DIRECTORY

A "metallic" is, strictly speaking, not a color but a specific type of shiny texture which can be applied to almost any color. It is usually created by using metal oxides with pigment to make glazes, inks and dyes for use on wall tiles and painted surfaces and for printing on wallcoverings and fabrics.

This type of texture is usually light-reflecting, with an attractive glint or gleam which makes the surface look brighter, richer, stronger and more "important," and it makes any pattern stand out. As with bold colors, shiny metallic effects can be disturbing and distracting, and should be used with care.

Gold, brass and copper can be classed as warm, and they work in a similar way to the advancing colors of the spectrum. Real gold and gold leaf are, of course, costly and precious; however, gold can now be simulated in paints and glazes. Brass and copper are far less costly than gold and can also be recreated using pigments and glazes.

In contrast, silver, platinum, steel, pewter and chrome have a coolness — in some cases, an almost icy effect — which relates to, and works in a color scheme in a similar way to pale gray. They tend to recede, and their shiny surface reflects light, visually increasing the apparent size of a space.

Gloss-glazed wall tiles
These can be combined with coordinating plain, similarly glazed field tiles to form a pattern, border or as drop-ins. [Country Floors]

American glazed tiles
The metallic "oilslick" look produces sophisticated wall treatments. The snail and shell raised motif is astonishingly realistic – will they leave a shiny trail? [Country Floors]

Handmade glazed wall tiles
Bronze autumnal colors are inset with relief-decorated tiles depicting frogs, toads, turtles, lizards, chameleons and fish, with a delicate tracery of leaves on other tiles to create an almost fossilized look. Use as drop-ins or to form a regular pattern; the frog-and-vine makes an effective border design. [Ann Sacks]

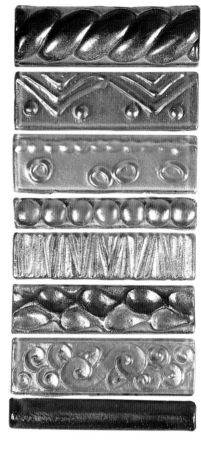

Molded glazed motif tiles
These border tiles are glazed with a rich bronze and golden metallic finish. They can be used to create decorative edging or framing, or combined with other tiles to form panels, dados, etc. [Hastings]

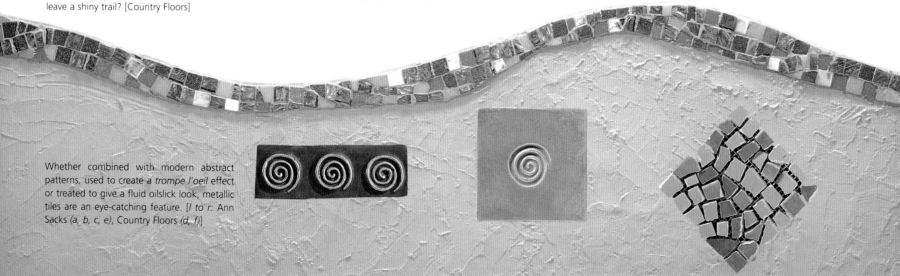

Whether combined with modern abstract patterns, used to create a *trompe l'oeil* effect or treated to give a fluid oilslick look, metallic tiles are an eye-catching feature. [*l to r*: Ann Sacks (*a, b, c, e*), Country Floors (*d, f*)]

Glazed ceramic tiles

The pattern forms a textured medallion design associated with classical European architecture. They can be used on interior or exterior walls (though not in a cold climate), fireplaces, etc., for dramatic light-reflecting effect. [Ann Sacks]

Italian glazed wall tiles

These tiles create a mosaic effect in "designer" colors. Here, they are set diamond-fashion for dramatic impact. [Hastings]

American glazed wall tiles

Field tiles in jewel-rich colors combined with shell-shaped relief molding can be hung to form a bold horizontal effect or used as a border/liner or frame. [Country Floors]

Glazed wall tiles

The bronze-bright and jewel-rich colors are combined with square mosaics used as drop-ins to create an exotic effect for walls in bathrooms, bedrooms or commercial situations. [Country Floors]

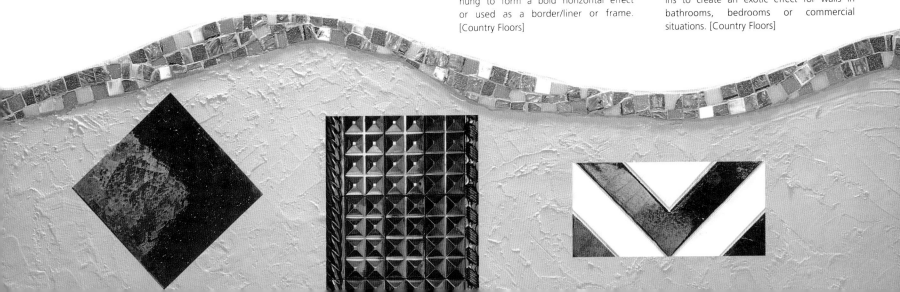

PRACTICAL
POINTERS

SURFACE SELECTION

For a really hardwearing and easy-to-clean surface, tiles are often the sensible option. But tiles can come in several different guises — from carpet and vinyl tiles, to rustic quarries and paving slabs. This book is concerned with "hard" flooring and walling which is usually seen as a permanent or at least long-lasting feature. Bear this in mind when making design and color choices.

Always make sure the tile you choose is suitable for the job. Floor tiles are stronger, thicker and usually larger than wall tiles. They may have substances added to the clay (limestone or flint chippings, silica, etc.) to make them tougher, and this may add a slight glitter to the texture when the tile has been fired. They are also heavier than many other floorings, or wall tiles, and consequently can create problems if used upstairs in an old property or in a conversion. First make sure the joists are strong enough (and have them strengthened if necessary) to take extra weight. Floor tiles for use in conservatories, porches, verandas, front paths and patios may need to have a visual link with the main house. They must be frostproof, i.e. fired to a sufficiently high temperature to withstand cold and frost and remove the possibility of cracking or breaking up.

Wall tiles are different from floor tiles. They are generally made of earthenware or white "china" clays and have a decorative (hand-decorated, printed, molded, etc.) or plain glazed surface. Although there are certain "standard" sizes, they come in a variety of different sizes, and some come in original shapes.

▲ This traditional treatment for a front pathway makes full use of frostproof quarry tiles, laid in a bold geometric pattern. The design could be echoed on the hall floor in this Victorian house. [H & R Johnson]

◄ Venetian marble slabs are laid diamond-fashion to "frame" a curvaceously shaped indoor pool. Floors in such areas must be impervious to water and non-slip. [Fired Earth]

There are also small "insets" or "drop-ins" which are used as an integral part of designs.

Wall tiles should never be used as flooring because they are not strong enough. In some cases, perhaps where continuity is required, floor tiles can be used on the wall. However, they are heavier, thicker — and so reduce the space — and are often more clumsy. Many manufacturers produce a wide choice of coordinating floor and wall tiles, which could be a better option for a seamless look.

There are also tiles produced specifically to be used as countertops, which are heavier than a simple laminate top. Kitchen, bathroom and bedroom furniture carcasses may therefore need to be strengthened at the joints to take the extra weight. Tiles for countertops must be impervious to oils, acids and other cooking liquids to be hygienic, so do not choose tiles with any porosity or with a "crackle" glaze. In some instances, unglazed floor tiles may be suitable for work surfaces if a special epoxy grout is used and they are properly sealed and maintained — ask the supplier for advice.

Finishes

Highly glazed and glossy tiles, and those with a luster (shiny) finish, are only suitable for use on walls and some work surfaces, as they would be highly dangerous on floors; the majority of floor tiles are matte or semi-matte for obvious reasons.

Tiles can also be textured for extra visual and tactile interest, and also as an extra safety factor for floors. However, dirt can become trapped in deep indentations and cleaning may be difficult. Floor tiles with a rustic texture are suitable for a country or Mediterranean-style room. Tiles of stone, slate, etc., can have a special riven surface — a slight texturing which makes them non-slip — but again, cleaning may be harder.

DESIGN OPTIONS

As most tiles are a regular shape (usually rectangular or square), there are endless design possibilities with plain colors, before patterned tiles are even contemplated. For example, light and dark colored floor tiles laid in a chessboard design will always look elegant and will help to make a small floor look larger, and increase the apparent size of the whole room.

Tiles can also be laid to form specific geometric patterns. This may be done by clever placing of plain tiles, or setting them diamond-fashion, or using different sizes to form a border effect to outline a room or salient feature. Tiles can be installed to create striped effects, either horizontally, vertically or diagonally. Tiles can also be cut diagonally to produce triangles, to extend geometric possibilities.

Alternatively, tiles can be set to graduate softly down the wall or across the floor in a monochromatic effect; starting with rows of pale tiles at the top of a wall, and working down to darker tones of the same color, can be a very stylish treatment. A patchwork effect using single, or even old tiles, can create an unusual

▷ Small encaustic insets add interest to plain glazed floor tiles in a farmhouse kitchen. [Fired Earth]

◁ Plain tiles can be used to create amazing geometric patterns. Such designs work best on a large, unbroken area of wall or floor. [Langley]

feature. Always try to combine tiles from the same range, or at least from the same manufacturer. If this is impossible, make sure the thickness and weight of the tiles is uniform.

Tiles are individually produced. Many handmade and hand-decorated tiles, or those with a dense color, can have slight variation in tone and/or color from different firings. It is therefore essential to get the tiler or flooring contractor (or you if you are doing it yourself) to "shuffle the pack." Open all the boxes or pallets and use the tiles at random, so any inconsistencies are lost when spread across a large area.

Pattern – and Plain

Tiles come in a baffling selection of designs and colors. Border and motif tiles can be set at the top, or across an area of plain tiles, or used to outline a salient feature. Motif tiles can be placed randomly throughout a run of plain or textured tiles for extra visual interest (although this often does not look as exciting as hoped!).

Tiles can also be produced to build up a pattern to cover an entire area, and can be floral, geometric, narrative, etc., or have a particular "period" flavor. Choose these to suit the architectural and decorative style of the room (some ranges are produced to coordinate specifically with wallcoverings and fabrics). There are also sets of tiles which form a complete picture, known as "panels." They may be sold already boxed, or made to order. Panels can make an interesting feature on a blank wall, and work particularly well in a windowless bathroom. Mural patterns can also be designed to order and look very effective around a swimming pool, in a dreary hall or in a commercial situation.

Most plain tiles have a solid-color effect created by the glaze, or are composed of a natural material which gives its own color to the tile. There are a wide variety available

Be Bold with Borders
Some tiles are specifically designed to be used as borders to "neaten" or create a "frame" on a plain wall, or to outline and define a feature. They can be strongly geometric [A, B, E] or flowingly floral [C, D]. Choose the pattern to suit the style of the room and the rest of the decorations.

Design a Border using Plain Tiles
Plain tiles can also be cut in a variety of shapes and hung in different ways to add impact and form borders, frames or panels [F, G, H].

A

B

C

D

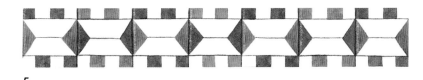

E

F

G

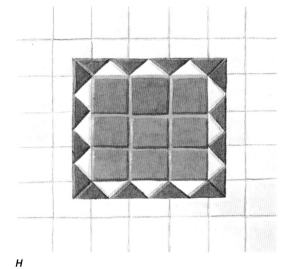

H

Stylish Shapes for Flooring

The regular module of tiles makes designing a fabulous floor much easier. Shown here are a few possibilities from herringbone and brick effect [C, G, J] to the classic way of combining a square or octagonal tile with a key square as an inset [B, E, F, K]. The tiles can be combined with a border [A] for extra definition, and can be laid in a diamond-trellis fashion [F, I, K]. Lozenge-shaped tiles [D, H] look dramatic even if they are laid in a conventional way.

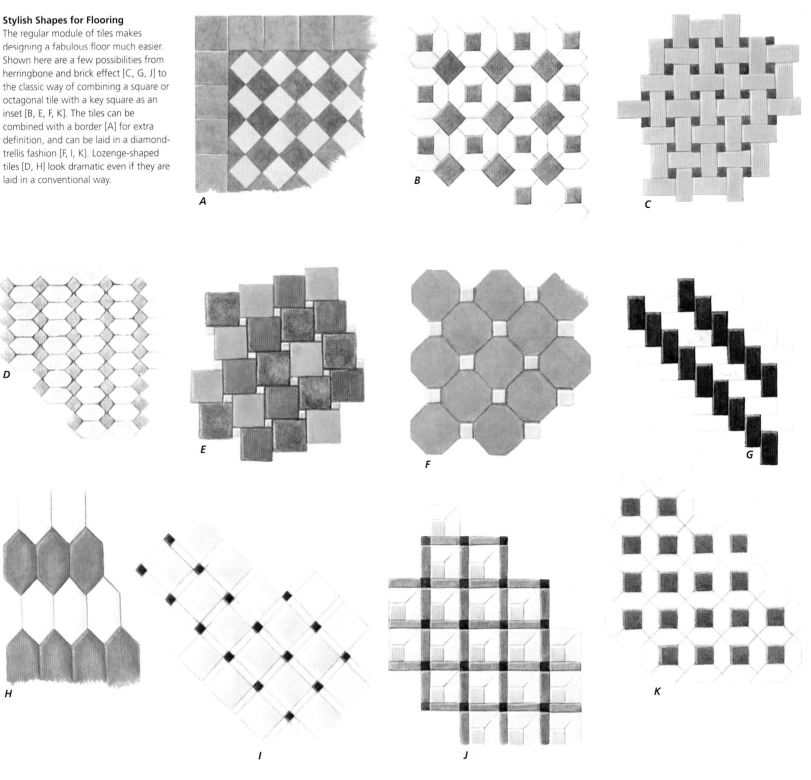

A

B

C

D

E

F

G

H

I

J

K

which allows many design possibilities. Many stippled, marbled, dragged, water-splashed and shadow-stripe effects are produced as an alternative to solid color to create a slightly larger effect – they are good for walls in a small bathroom.

Look before you Leap

Remember that bold designs and strong colors seem more intrusive when used over a large wall or floor area. (They can have the visual effect of "falling in" on you or coming up towards you.) The paler colors and softer patterns tend to fade into insignificance and are unobtrusive when used in bulk. Try to follow the color rule of relating the scale of pattern or strength of color to the size of the surface on which it is to be used. Showrooms have tile displays, which help you to judge the finished effect, such as pull-out display boards for walls and trays for floors. Special mirrored boxes or mirrored panels help to magnify the effect of several tiles used together, so a whole wall or floor can be assessed.

When selecting tiles, take samples of existing items in the room (bathroom equipment, kitchen cabinets, fabrics, etc.) with you. If this is not possible or practical, ask to take a tile or two home with you to check *in situ*. Look at them on the correct plane – wall tiles against the wall and floor tiles down on the floor – and under exact lighting conditions, both day and night.

◀ A cool blue hand-painted traditional *trompe l'oeil* tile panel would look fresh and elegant in a kitchen, bathroom, hall, dining room or conservatory, adding visual interest without being too overpowering. [Castelnau Tiles]

◀ Different tones of natural terracotta floor tiles are laid in a diamond design to increase the width of the space visually, and bordered to suggest a rug – a good treatment to break up a long narrow floor area. [Sussex Terracotta]

PREPARATION – THE UNDERPINNINGS

As with all interior decoration, the finished job will only be as good as the initial preparation. This applies not only to the surface on which you will lay floor tiles, or hang wall tiles, but more essentially to structural problems – damp or dry rot must be dealt with first, for instance. If an area is damp, a permanent floor treatment could form an impervious barrier and cause condensation (rising damp) to creep up the walls, or damp walls may crumble and the tiles fall off!

Hard (permanent) flooring – such as tiles, stone, marble, slate, earthenware *carrés*, etc. – is very heavy. When combined with a large cast-iron bath filled with water, or used in a kitchen with massive units and hefty kitchen appliances, their weight becomes an even more important factor. If this type of floor is contemplated in a conversion, or for an upstairs room in an older property, the floor joists should always be checked first to make sure they can bear the extra weight and, if necessary, be strengthened. In many older properties, floorboards and joists are narrower the higher they are positioned in the house – the servants living in the uppermost rooms were provided with only essential furniture!

When you contemplate tiling a wall or floor area, think carefully about any other work which might be carried out. Installing new lighting may involve embedding cable in the wall, or replumbing can lead to new pipe runs. If possible, do not embed cables or pipes under permanent flooring because if something goes wrong, the whole floor may have to be excavated to find the fault. (There are electronic devices which detect faults, but they are not always accurate.) It is wiser to run cables or pipes around the edge of the floor and conceal them behind panels, or cover with some boxing-in.

When tiling walls, avoid hiding electric cables behind, or having switches and controls combined with, the tiled wall area. To overcome this problem, a paneled "inspection hatch" could be made and tiled to match the rest of the wall. It is also worth adding a panel around the bath or basin, and then tiling it to match the wall area. This creates a neat, seamless look and visually increases the size of the room. These panels need to be constructed so they can be removed easily if you are faced with plumbing problems.

What Goes on Top of What – Walls
Before hanging tiles, the surface must be level, smooth and free from grease and dust. You may be presented with a variety of wall surfaces to prepare:

Plastered walls can usually be tiled. Leave new plaster to dry for at least one month before tiling, and then seal with tile adhesive primer. Old plaster can be sanded and any cracks filled. Allow the putty (filler) to dry before tiling, and if it covers a large area, prime with tile adhesive primer.

Wallboard (plasterboard) can be tiled if it is firm and on a solid framework, but do not use very heavy tiles. Treat as for a plastered or painted wall.

Painted walls can usually be tiled, but may need to be "keyed" first. Make sure the paint is firmly stuck to the wall. Remove any hooks, nails, etc., and pull out any old anchors (wallplugs), fill any holes, and sand any bumps. Any "suspect" area of painted surface (which has been subject to damp, efflorescence, etc., or is flaky or powdery) should be sealed with tile adhesive primer. Use sandpaper to reduce gloss paint to a matte surface, and then wash with sugar soap. Treat latex emulsion paint or distemper similarly, and then, using the corner of a paint scraper, score the entire surface in a 4in (10cm) wide criss-cross pattern. This keyed surface ensures that the adhesive bonds with the wall. Seal with tile adhesive primer if necessary.

Wallpapered walls are unsuitable for tiling (including heavier, embossed papers and painted woodchip paper). All wallpaper must be completely stripped and any cracks filled. Sand the surface and wash with sugar soap and, if necessary, coat with tile adhesive primer. Lining or cross-lining walls is not recommended before tiling.

Paneled walls are usually not suitable for tiling. However, special blockboard or water-and-boil-proof (WBP) plywood panels can be made, for where you want to have access to the wall behind. These need not be beautifully finished but must be stable; any bare wood frame should be primed with oil-based primer.

Wood paneling that has been tiled may not remain stable, so it is best to remove it. Hardboard is too flimsy to tile, and chipboard and insulation board swell when wet. Prepare the area behind the paneling according to its surface (wood cladding is sometimes used to cover old tiles!).

Existing tiles – it is possible to tile on top of existing tiles as long as they are firmly adhered. The wall should be thoroughly checked first – if the new tiles are very heavy, they could pull the old tiles off the wall! If the wall is solid, remove any cracked or loose tiles and level the cavity with putty (filler). "Key" (rub firmly) the surface with a coarse silicon carbide paper and then wash with sugar soap. Tile adhesive used on a previously tiled surface takes longer to dry than on a plastered or painted wall, so leave the tiles for a longer period before grouting (about 3–4 days). In this situation, self-spacing "Universal" tiles with several beveled glazed edges are practical and easier to hang.

What Goes on Top of What – Floors
In the main, floors should be professionally laid, which means calling in a flooring contractor to advise, estimate and then possibly carry out the work. Many suppliers, importers and manufacturers can recommend suitable contractors, and some will actually do the work. As with all decorating jobs, it is wise to obtain at least two or three estimates. Before booking the work force, ask how long the work will take to carry out, as well as cost; also ask for

Exotic classical patterns on glazed wall and floor tiles create a raised Turkish-style bathing area, reminiscent of the Islamic tiled walls seen in harems and palaces in the Middle East in the 17th and 18th centuries. Young men "doing the grand tour" were inspired by such treatments and copied them when they returned home and refurbished their historic houses and mansions. [World's End Tiles]

recommendations from a few satisfied customers, unless the supplier has suggested the contractor.

Concrete or cement floors can usually be laid directly onto the surface if it is smooth, level and clean. In some cases, for instance if the floor is uneven, floor-leveling compound may need to be applied first.

Direct-to-earth Some older properties do not have suspended floors, and flagstones were usually laid directly on the earth. This can

still be done if the area is level and free from damp, although screeding may be more satisfactory. Quarry tiles are usually laid in a mortar bed, so are particularly suitable in this situation.

Wooden suspended floorboards cannot have tiles laid directly on top. Wood can warp, and the tiles could crack with the movement. Wooden floors need to be covered with a ½in (15mm) of exterior grade plywood, which will stand up to the moisture in the adhesive. This should be "staggered" so it does not line up

with the boards, and if necessary "inspection hatches" should be provided. Some wooden floorings, such as parquet tiles, may already be laid on top of a concrete or cement base; floorboards are usually fixed to wooden joists. It is better to take these up and start from scratch.

Vinyl and linoleum can have tiles laid on top if the original subfloor is in good condition, and the main floor is properly stuck down and is clean and level. Vinyl and lino must be treated first with a special primer.

Old tiles and flagstones, etc. It may be possible to restore a floor which is already tiled by replacing broken, cracked or worn tiles or stones. If this is not feasible, and you are proposing to renew the hard flooring completely, do not pour floor-leveling compound or a new hard base on top – it is far better to have it taken up professionally for salvage. The reclaimed floor may be exactly what someone else is looking for, and you will have more in your budget from the sale of the old floor to put towards your new one.

WHEN TO DO IT YOURSELF

When it comes to the actual physical work, it is always best to be realistic and admit your limitations! Tiling a floor is heavy work, but tiling walls and work surfaces are both well within the capability of the average handy person and can be very satisfying to do.

Walls are not particularly difficult to tile and tiling a work surface should be even easier. Your experience, together with the information in this book, will tell you which surfaces you can and cannot tile. So both jobs can be tackled yourself, as long as you remember the following golden rules. Start with a suitable surface – clean, smooth and dry; purchase the right sort and correct number of tiles; use the right tools for the job. Make sure you have the correct quantities of tiles as well as suitable adhesive and grout to finish the job.

Laying Floorings

Tiling floors is heavy work. Bearing in mind this type of hard flooring usually becomes a permanent and integral part of the building, you do not want to make a mistake, and may decide to call in the professionals. A specialist flooring contractor is probably the preferred option, although many builders are qualified to lay most types of hard flooring. Some suppliers of tile, slate, stone, etc., have a supply-design-and-lay service; others can often recommend suitable contractors in your area.

Many of the conservatory, kitchen and bathroom specialists who offer a "package" of design-build-and-install also offer to lay floor tiles and hang wall tiles. Others consider this to be part of the decoration or finishing of the room, and do not include it in their service. Always check to see exactly what is on offer – a quote may be cheaper from one source than another because they do not decorate, hang tiles or lay flooring.

▶ An interesting, almost textured, effect is created by the clever use of stoneware floor tiles in warm natural colors. Such a complex design, using weighty tiles, is a job best left to the experts. [Metropolitan Tile Company]

Quarries and some ceramic tiles could be installed yourself, although quarry tiles need to be laid in a mortar bed, which is hard work to prepare. In the main, it is best to leave marble, slate, natural stone, earthenware slabs, flagstones, granite, etc., to be laid by the experts. A professional will also make sure the subfloor is suitable – and if necessary level, re-screed or strengthen it, and should also know the correct adhesives, grout and final dressing to use. If laying a floor yourself, check the right materials to use with the manufacturer or supplier. Do not forget that final dressings should always be non-slip.

When laying a floor yourself, consider your method of working so you do not "box yourself" into the room! You will need to leave the room and shut the door while the tiles "settle," and the mortar or adhesives and grout dry (sometimes this can take about three days). With the design worked out in advance, lay out the tiles accordingly. Always start at the corner farthest from the door and work backwards towards the exit.

Designing Floors and Walls

If you do not have the confidence to design a floor or wall yourself, there are experts who can do it for you. Many tile suppliers and specialist makers and studios will work out individual designs; they can even create and decorate tiles for a unique look or a *trompe l'oeil* mural effect. Some of the specialist contractors, suppliers and manufacturers provide a design service using CAD (computer-aided design), and produce a printout to scale, together with quantities of the tiles needed.

Alternatively, a professional interior designer can take the burden off your shoulders. They prefer to work from the floor up because the floor is one of the most permanent areas in a room, and all other surfaces are seen in relation to it, as well as the furniture standing on it. They usually ask lots of questions to establish your needs and requirements – including the available budget. They will measure and then produce sample boards and plans, and a rough idea of costs. Once you approve the designs, they obtain firm quotes from the suppliers and work force, and then order the materials. Ask them to obtain quotes for the time the job is likely to take, as well as cost. Most interior designers will supervise every stage of structural and decorating work, so if the job is likely to be messy, this may be a wise opportunity to take a short trip away from home!

For a floor or wall which is to have a special pattern or design set into it, the designer will usually submit detailed plans and/or elevations as well as sketches. If you are undecided about the way a specific design will work, ask them to provide some alternative suggestions. The designer will probably provide them on a separate overlay so you can judge the full effect by placing it over the top of the scale floor plan or wall elevations.

PLANNING THE DESIGN

Plan the effect of a tiled area on paper first. This means you can make alterations without making mistakes, and it also helps to work out the quantities of tiles required. If you are having a professionally designed floor or wall installed, the supplier may use CAD (computer-aided design). You may have the opportunity to see the finished effect on screen, and you will be given a printout, together with a list of the quantities of tiles required. Always order a few spare tiles to allow for accidents or mistakes!

However, in the absence of CAD, experimenting on paper can help if you are undecided on a particular effect or way of grouping tiles. Look at these designs in the room which is to be tiled, and discuss them with other family members (if relevant). It may be useful to draw a scale plan of the wall or floor area to be tiled on squared or graph paper, and to try out different effects on tracing paper overlays.

Start by measuring accurately and preparing the basic plans (do this yourself, even if you have an architect's or builder's plan). Make a floor plan: this is a flat plan which represents a room looking down from above. It needs to contain the exact positions of doors (and door "swings" to show which way they open), windows, alcoves, recesses and projections (such as a chimney breast), radiators, built-in furniture, plumbing positions and electric points, etc.

If the walls are to be tiled, make wall elevations for each wall – these are similar flat plans of walls with any important fixtures such as windows, doors, etc., drawn to scale in the correct position. These plans are invaluable for tiling around windows, doors and other features.

Equipment

In order to measure accurately, you will need a 5- or 7-yard (meter) retractable steel tape (fabric tapemeasures stretch with use!), a plumb line, a spirit level, a T-square, sketch pad, pencils and pens.

To draw the finished plans, you will need a ruler (preferably a scale rule), a set square (to ensure accurate angles), a pair of compasses (to draw curves/door swings), pencils, a drawing pen or good-quality ballpoint, squared or graph paper, and detail or tracing paper for the finished plan and/or overlays.

Measuring

It helps to have another person to assist – to hold the other end of the tape, and perhaps to cross-check your measurements or call them out for you to write down. First sketch a rough plan of the room and the walls – at this stage it does not need to be accurate. Then measure accurately and write the measurements on the plan. Start at one corner of the room and work outwards from it. When measuring, keep the measure taut, and to make sure you have the true vertical and true horizontal, use the spirit level and plumb line. Ideally, take the horizontal measurements at ground level.

Measure the depth and height of baseboards (skirting), dados and dado rails, window frames, depth and width of sills, height of windows from the floor, doors and door frames, window frames, architraves, etc.; mark exact positions of built-in furniture, electric outlets (points) and pipes. Also take diagonal measurements across both walls and floors, to help check the final plan.

Choose a scale to work in, making one square on the paper equal to one unit of measurement, and transfer the measurements from your rough drawing to squared paper. Use a pencil first, and when you are satisfied the plan is correct, draw it in ink. For the **floor plan**, draw the shape of the room accurately in your chosen scale. When working in metric, a scale of 1:25 or 1:50 is usual, but if you are using standard (imperial) measurements, make one foot of floor space equal to 1in or ½in on the paper (i.e. a scale of 1:12 or 1:24). Indicate any projections, recesses, etc. Use the compasses to draw curves (door swings) and the set square for neat angles.

Using the same scale as for the floor plans, draw the **wall elevations** in a similar way. Include the exact

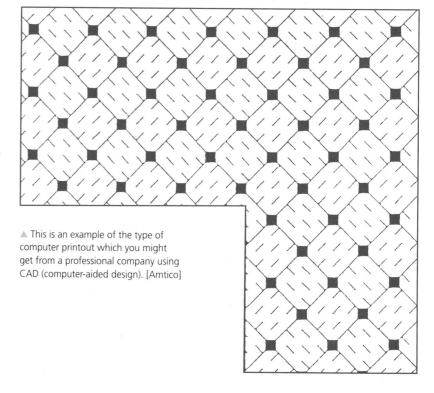

▲ This is an example of the type of computer printout which you might get from a professional company using CAD (computer-aided design). [Amtico]

position of windows, doors, built-in furniture and any items which are seen against the wall, e.g. a sink, kitchen units, bath (allow for any paneling [boxing-in] of such items).

Use this plan to figure out the floor or wall tile pattern. Take several photocopies to use for rough initial planning; you can then trace your design onto plain tracing paper, and use colored pencils to indicate the finished effect. By using a transparent acetate or tracing paper overlay, you can work out the best way to position the tiles to avoid difficult edges or an awkwardly placed motif. Always center a pattern or motif on an architectural feature in the same way as you would with wallpaper. When planning a very complicated design, it is worthwhile working to a scale of one square on the paper equal to one tile. With an accurate plan and design completed, you can then figure out the exact quantities of tiles required.

Estimating Quantities

First of all, check the size of tile to be used. There are "standard" square or rectangular tiles, but imported tiles may be of a different shape and size. There are different shapes – octagonal, lozenge, special interlocking shapes and triangular (although it is more usual to cut a square tile across the diagonal if you

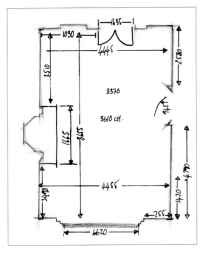

▲ Sketch a floor plan and mark on all the relevant measurements. Use a compass to draw the door swings and do not forget to include architectural features.

Draw a plan (called an elevation) of each wall. First, multiply the width and height (A) to establish the total area. Do the same to calculate the area taken up by doors (B); windows (C); and other architectural features (D). Subtract these from the total wall area to find the space to be tiled. Divide this by the area of each tile to calculate the number of tiles. Allow for wastage due to awkward areas.

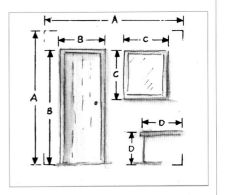

want to use triangles). Border tiles (designed to go at the top of a run of tiles) are usually narrow in depth, but they relate in width to the tiles with which they are used.

Always make sure you buy enough tiles to complete the job, and check that they are from the same "batch" or firing (there is usually a batch number printed on the box); the color can vary dramatically from one firing to another.

Standard wall tile sizes are 4 x 4in (100 x 100mm); 4¼ x 4¼in (108 x 108mm) – the traditional British bathroom size; 6 x 6in (152 x 152mm); 6 x 8in (152 x 203mm); 8 x 8in (203 x 203mm); 8 x 10in (203 x 250mm); 8 x 12in (203 x 300mm).

There are several *faux* mosaic tile brands available. These are standard-size tiles textured and scored to look like a mosaic and hung as conventional tiles.

Mosaic tiles are much smaller. They can be 1 x 1in (25 x 25mm) or 2 x 2in (50 x 50mm), but they usually come as panels on a fiber-mesh backing. They are installed by embedding the backing into the adhesive or, alternatively, they may have a paper facing which can be removed easily after setting the mosaics in place.

The panels usually measure 10 x 10in (250 x 250mm) or 12 x 12in (300 x 300mm), overall measurements which can be used to calculate quantities.

If the smaller-sized mosaic tiles are not available separately, they can be removed from the backing of a panel and used individually. They can be used as drop-ins to form a "key square" – combined with octagonal-shaped plain tiles, usually in a contrasting color to add decorative interest – a very traditional way of laying tiles, especially on floors. Always make sure drop-ins and field tiles are designed to be used together – depth, glaze, size, etc., must all be compatible.

Small floor tile sizes are: 6 x 4in (152 x 100mm); 6 x 6in (152 x 152mm) (quarries); 8 x 6in (200 x 152mm); 8 x 8in (200 x 200mm) upwards.

Some stone, slate, etc., tiles can be as large as 10 x 16in (280 x 400mm) or 12 x 12in (300 x 300mm). Older flagstones and reclaimed earthenware tiles can be even larger – up to 18 x 18in (500 x 500mm) and beyond, so always double-check the size of the tiles before you start working out patterns and effects on squared paper, or trying to calculate quantities.

A tiled wall needs neat edges. To half- or part-tile and finish with a border is simple enough. With ordinary square tiles, use fully glazed edges on exposed sides. "Universal" or self-spacing tiles have several beveled, glazed edges so they can be used for corners and edges.

This problem rarely occurs with floor tiles, as they butt right up to the baseboard (skirting). Where floors join at a doorway, they may need to be combined with a threshold. There are several different types, made from metal or wood. Wooden thresholds can be colored to coordinate with the flooring, or special slim linking tiles are available.

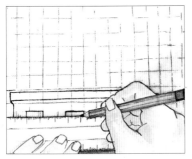

Draw a plan of each section of wall to be tiled; ideally, one square will equal one tile.

Draw the design on the plan. Use pencil first so that you can erase mistakes.

CUTTING TILES

Most tiling jobs will involve cutting and possibly drilling the tiles. Wall tiles are fairly easy to cut; floor tiles are harder. Learning to do this takes a little practice, and there may be a few breakages, so make sure you have enough spare tiles to allow for mistakes! Glazed tiles are vitrified, and cut edges can be very sharp, so it is wise to wear gloves when cutting tiles.

Most wall tiles have a glazed surface and are fairly brittle. Once the glazed surface has been scored, the tile should snap easily along the scored line. Mark the glazed side of the tile where it is to be cut using a metal straightedge and then score it with a tile cutter. You should wear protective gloves. Never mark the back of a tile with a felt pen or marker, as the clay can absorb the color and seep through to the front of the tile. The traditional technique is then to place a matchstick under the back of the tile, level with the scored line, and to press firmly on each side of the tile to achieve a clean cut. Alternatively, a tile-cutting jig has a built-in marking gauge – it should come with full instructions.

To cut a tile to fit around a light switch, window frame or pipe, draw and score the shape in the same way and then "nibble" away the excess with pincers, or use a tile-cutting hacksaw blade. Any rough edges can then be smoothed with a carborundum stone or tile file. To cut a square or oblong shape from the corner of a tile, first score the outline of the piece to be cut; then score criss-cross lines across the portion of tile which is to be removed – this makes it easier to cut away the excess with pincers or clippers.

Using a tile saw is easier than "nibbling" the tile away with pincers, but it has a very sharp blade. The tile must be supported carefully on a firm surface, with the part to be cut away projecting over the edge. In some cases, it is advisable to use the tile saw in conjunction with a vise or special work bench, in which case the tile should be padded to prevent shattering. Another type of specialist cutter has a cutting wheel to score the glaze, and jaws to hold the tile; when the handles are squeezed, the jaws close and break the tile. One of the easiest ways to cut a round shape accurately in the center of a tile is to make a template from brown paper or cardboard first. Trace the outline onto the tile, cut it in half and then "nibble" or cut away the two semicircles to make the hole for a pipe or light switch.

There are specialist profiling tools to help take an impression of difficult shapes; movable plastic or metal "teeth" mold around any shape they are pressed against, to give an accurate guide. This is very useful for awkward molded architraves, window frames, the sides of a basin, etc. You can use them to draw the shape directly onto the tiles, or to make a template first.

CUTTING A TILE INTO TWO PIECES

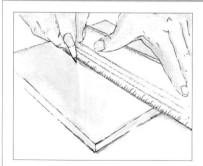

Use a ruler to score a straight line along the glazed side of the tile with a tile cutter.

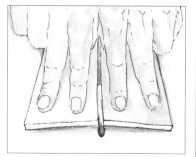

Place a matchstick underneath the scored line. Press the edges of the tile to break it.

CUTTING OUT SHAPES WITH STRAIGHT EDGES

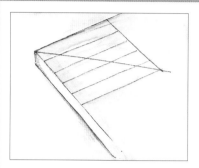

Score the outer edges of the shape to be cut, then score diagonally across the area.

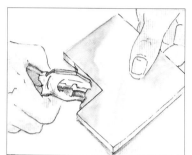

Use pincers to nibble away the corner and then smooth the cut edges.

CUTTING OUT SHAPES WITH CURVED EDGES

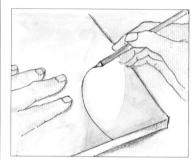

Draw the shape to be cut onto a cardboard template and copy this onto the tile. Score.

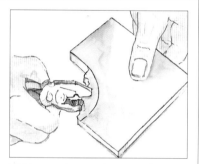

Nibble away the curved corner with a pair of pincers and then smooth the cut edges.

CUTTING OUT A CIRCLE IN THE CENTER OF A TILE

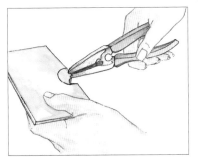

Score and break the tile in half. Draw a semicircle onto each half with a template.

Use pincers to nibble away the semicircles. Place the two tiles back together.

DRILLING HOLES IN TILES

Place masking tape over the areas to be drilled to stop the drill from slipping.

If you need to drill a hole in a ceramic tile, do this after the tile is in position. Measure and mark the point to be drilled and stick masking tape over the marks to prevent the bit from slipping. Use a special spade-shaped tile bit on the drill and switch to a low speed; protect your eyes, face and hands from the powdered glaze/glass which flies off.

Floor Tiles

Floor tiles are much harder to cut than wall tiles. An ordinary wall tile cutter cannot be used, although a stout tile saw is adequate for cutting out small pieces (clamp the tile in a vise or special work bench with protective padding). You will need to purchase or rent a special floor tile cutter, or if you are working with thick tiles (quarries, etc.), you will need a professional tile cutter. These can usually be rented from specialist shops, or sometimes from tile suppliers and hardware stores (DIY shops). If renting tools, make sure they come with full operating instructions.

For very heavy tiles and quarries, an angle grinder is the best tool to use and is available to rent. These need careful handling; always wear protective clothing, including boots, and support the tile on a stout surface. Do not put the grinder down until the wheel has stopped.

◀ A selection of natural terracotta tiles in rich earth colors for floors and work surfaces – such tiles are thicker and tougher than wall tiles and are much harder to cut, so this is a job often best left to an expert. [Société Carré]

GROUTING TILES

Grout is the essential finishing touch to most tiled surfaces; it prevents water and other liquids and dirt from penetrating the gaps between the tiles. The tiles are grouted after they have been in place for about 12–48 hours (refer to the adhesive package for the recommended time) and the adhesive is set. Grout is usually a neutral color, but it is possible to purchase colored grout, or to color it yourself, if the lines formed by the tiles are intended to be an integral part of the finished design.

Grout comes either in powder form or ready-mixed in a tub. Powder needs to be mixed in a bucket to a fairly stiff and smooth consistency, according to the manufacturer's instructions. Ready-mixed grout needs to be stirred well, and replace the lid when it is not being used. Make sure you have enough grout, but if you are using powder, do not mix too much if the job is being done in several stages. Work as quickly as possible, as grout hardens rapidly.

There are different types of grout; always make sure you use the right one for the job. For example, a special epoxy grout must be used for countertops because it is impervious to cooking "spills" and acids. This type is also often recommended for floors for hygiene reasons. As grouting can be a messy job, always cover nearby surfaces before starting (bath, sink, kitchen units, etc.). Remove spacers or matchsticks if you have used them. Using a special grout spreader, rubber squeegee blade or damp sponge, spread the grout over the tiled surface. Work quickly, pressing the grout well into the gaps. Do not let the grout harden on the front of the tiles – wipe away any excess with a damp sponge, wash out frequently to avoid smears. When using epoxy grout, use a spatular to remove the excess. When the grout has begun to harden, run a rounded stick between the joints to smooth them off and make sure there are no gaps. At the same time, check for any grout left on the tiles and remove it at once. When tiles butt up to an adjoining surface (e.g. a bath, sink, countertop, etc.), do not grout along the joining line, which needs to be sealed with a silicone or acrylic sealant after the grout has dried fully. Scrape out any grout which inadvertently falls into the gap.

The same method is applied when grouting a floor, starting from the corner farthest from the door, backwards towards the exit, and cleaning off the top of the tile as you go. As the grout hardens, run a piece of dowel between the joints to firm it in and check there are no air pockets. Leave to harden as recommended by the manufacturer.

When laying quarry tiles, it is best to seal them before grouting. Take advice on which sealant to use (two coats of thinned linseed oil is a popular option); grout and then rub with a coarse cloth. If there are grout stains on the top of the tiles, use sawdust to remove them – strew it over the floor, rub with a damp cloth, and sweep up the residue.

Design Tip

If you are not retiling, you can regrout an existing tiled wall, floor or work surface to give it a new lease of life. A change of color to define the tiles – to contrast or coordinate with them – can create an important design feature.

STANDARD GROUT

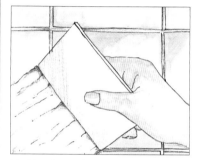

Working diagonally, spread grout across the tiled surface, pressing it into the gaps.

Drag a piece of doweling along the gaps between tiles to produce an even finish.

EPOXY GROUT

Press long, thin strips of grout into the gaps with the edge of the applicator.

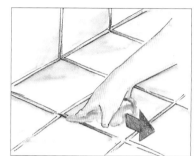

Rub along the edges with a soft, damp cloth. Always work in the same direction.

HOW TO TILE WALLS

A tiled wall is both beautiful and practical, and tiling a complete wall is not too difficult a job for the average handy person. However, if you have never done anything like this before, it is wise to begin with a simple and fairly small area such as a splashback, dado, etc. The secret of successful tiling lies in planning the job properly at the outset so that you can judge the effect before rushing out to buy boxes of tiles.

Always buy the best tools you can afford, and use and keep them safely – this applies for all do-it-yourself jobs. Before starting, make sure you have all the materials to complete the job – i.e. enough tiles, adhesive, grout, etc. – nothing is more frustrating than running out of materials halfway through a job!

Setting Out the Tiles

A successful tiled wall is set out so a pattern is easy on the eye, centered on any features (e.g. a window, basin, stove recess, chimney breast, etc.) and not "slipping off the wall," and has a good pattern match. Tiles should not have to be awkwardly cut.

To achieve this usually means starting in the center of a wall, or area to be tiled, and working out toward the edges with any cut pieces (of equal size) coming at the end of each row. This is fairly easy on a blank wall, but harder to achieve where there are projections, recesses or doors and windows to be accommodated.

Find the exact center (midpoint) of the wall to be tiled by measuring and drawing a central vertical line

with the aid of a plumb line. Lay out a row of tiles as a "dry run," placing a tile on each side of this line. If it looks awkward and will result in difficult cuts at each end of the row of tiles, you could center one tile on the midpoint. This is often the best

method when tiling splashbacks for a sink or behind the bath, centering a single tile on the midpoint behind the faucets.

Make a gauge or marking stick from a length of wood and mark it in the width of the tiles you are using. Hold it against the wall in various positions to see how the tiles fall. You can do this on both the horizontal and vertical plane, but you will have to make two different gauge sticks if the tiles are not square.

It is also essential to establish a level base – the bottom row of tiles must be level. This means working to the true horizontal, which may not necessarily be the same as the baseboard (skirting) or the floor! To get this right, use a batten and spirit level and draw a line right around the room.

Alternatively, lightly tack a lath to the wall, approximately one tile high from the floor. The line should not be more than the depth of the tile above the finishing point, and a spare tile can be used to check this. If the

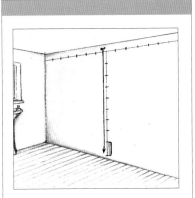

Use a plumb line (or weighted string) to find the true vertical line; use a spirit level to find the true horizontal line.

floor is uneven and the tiles will leave a gap, redraw the line or replace the lath. When tiling more than one wall, continue the line around the other walls, again checking with the spirit level at regular intervals.

If there are doors, windows, bathroom or kitchen appliances, pipes, etc., to be accommodated, figure out where the tiles will fall.

◄ Tiling around a window recess can be a very attractive and practical solution in a kitchen or bathroom where the window is above the sink. The simple geometric effect coordinates well with the pleated Roman shades used for the window. [Marlborough Tiles]

TILING A WALL USING BATTENS

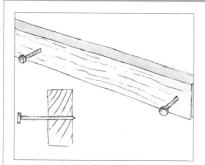

Mark the baseline on the wall. Drive nails partway through the wooden batten.

Place the batten level with the baseline and tap in the nails to hold it in place.

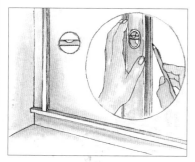

Figure out where the last whole tile will fall. Use a spirit level to mark this line.

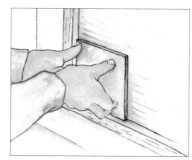

Attach a vertical batten in place and then start tiling where the two battens intersect.

When complete, remove adhesive from between the battens and tiles with a knife.

Remove the battens. Measure and cut tiles to fit into the spaces that are left.

TILING CORNERS

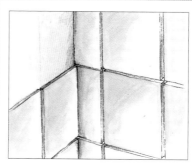

Overlap one tile over the other at internal corners; choose the least noticeable way.

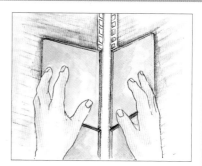

Finish external corners with a trim strip. Make sure the tiles on either side align.

TILING WINDOW RECESSES

Tile the wall before the recess. Arrange for equal size cuts at both ends of the sill.

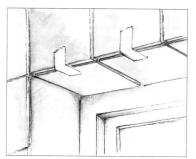

Tile the underside of the recess last. Tape the tiles for extra support.

Use the marking stick to measure the tile widths between the baseline and any fixtures; if the tile cuts will fall awkwardly, adjust the baseline or midpoint accordingly. Try to line tiles up with window frames (so the sill can also be neatly tiled) and to come level with bathtubs, etc.

You can use squared paper to see how the tiles will fall. This is especially practical if the wall to be tiled has lots of features, or the pattern will be complicated to match. Make one square equal to one tile.

Installing the Tiles

If you are using self-spacing or "Universal" tiles, you do not need to use matchsticks or tile spacers, but they will be necessary if the tiles do not have special beveled edges.

Use the recommended tile adhesive (a waterproof adhesive is essential for kitchens and bathrooms). Starting at the midpoint, spread the adhesive using a good notched spreader and lay the tiles in blocks of approximately 1 square yard/meter and work along the wall. (Start in a corner if the wall is blank and there are to be no tile cuts.) Use the back of the spreader to scoop the adhesive from the tub and spread it in an even layer ⅛in (2–3mm) thick, "combing" it with the notches on the spreader.

Start to set the tiles in place, aligning them with your batten or lath. If a sealing strip is to be positioned between a work surface (or bath) and the tiles, bed it into the adhesive before aligning the tiles with it. Push each tile firmly into position

on the adhesive, checking that it sits square with the aid of a plumb line and spirit level.

If you are using matchsticks or tile spacers, push these into the adhesive at the top and bottom of the tiles where they join. Complete the area, checking regularly that the tiles are square, level and flush. Continue until you have filled the area which can be covered with uncut tiles. Leave for 12–24 hours (or until the adhesive is dry) and then remove any laths and/or battens and pull out the spacers or matchsticks, reserving them for future use. Measure, cut and install tiles in the area around the edge of the tiling, or lay border tiles in position. When the adhesive has set, clean and grout the tiles.

HOW TO TILE A WORK SURFACE

Tiled countertops are a very practical finish for surfaces in the kitchen, bathroom, bedroom and children's rooms, and are relatively easy to install as the force of gravity is not working against you! For a seamless look, a single slab of granite, slate or marble can be used as a continuous top; but installation would be a job for the expert as its weight makes it difficult to handle.

A tiled top is also heavy, so first make sure the structure of the unit to be tiled is strong enough to take the weight. If necessary, reinforce the corner joints, backs and sides of kitchen, bedroom or bathroom units, or any other piece of furniture to be used, such as a chest of drawers, desk, table or washstand.

A tiled kitchen countertop will blunt knives and is not an ideal surface for rolling out pastry or for chopping food, but a chopping board or marble slab can be placed on top, or be inset into the surface. Decide the most practical and coolest position if it is to be integrated.

The edges of the tiled area can be finished with either edging tiles or wood. Edging tiles sometimes come as part of a standard work surface kit, complete with internal and external corner edge tiles. Hardwood may be chosen to link with units or furniture, or it could be colored to contrast and provide an extra design feature. However you finish edges, make sure it will be possible to open the top drawer of the units!

Tiles for a work surface should be at least ¼in (5mm) thick to withstand hot and heavy pans. They should not be too highly glazed since this surface is slippery. Most wall tiles are not suitable for a kitchen countertop, although they could be used in a bathroom or bedroom. Select tiles to use from the choice of special ones available, or some of the thinner floor tiles are also suitable. The work surface and floor could be tiled to coordinate. When tiling over an old tiled countertop, thinner tiles can be used.

The size of tile you choose is also a matter of personal taste. The smaller

FINDING THE "KEY" TILE

Plan the layout of the tiles carefully. A "key" tile – where the horizontal and vertical rows intersect – will become obvious.

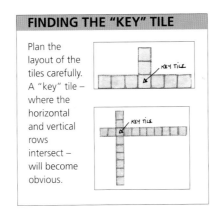

(4½ x 4½in/108 x 108mm) tiles are more complicated to work with, and tiles over 6 x 6in (150 x 150mm) can be more difficult to handle and may need cutting. In the main, the size of the surface to be tiled will influence your decision since it is better to cover as much of the surface as possible with uncut tiles. It is also visually pleasing to have the continuity of the same tiles on the wall and forming a splashback or curved upstand.

It is essential to use the right adhesive and grout. The adhesive should be of the "thin-bed" floor type and the best grout to use is an "epoxy grout," which is impervious to cooking liquids and germs and should be relatively stain-resistant. This type of grout has to be applied

▲ The cool blues and greens create a "patchwork" effect on the splashback above the blue tiled work surface. The tiles line up well across the two surfaces. [Société Carré]

with a spatula, rather than a sponge or squeegee.

A suitable, firm surface is needed to provide a "bed" for the tiles. Some cupboards may be covered already with wood or laminate which may be strong enough to tile over, but if necessary, screw supporting battens to the underside of the unit. Curved post-formed edges need to be cut square, or built up with wooden lipping and putty (filler). Metal edging should be removed; wooden lipping can either be tiled over or built up to form the edge of the new tiled work surface.

TILING A WORK SURFACE

If the edge of the work surface is to be trimmed with wood, nail a batten into position to act as a guide. The wooden trim should be attached after tiling is complete to avoid damaging it.

If the edge of the work surface is to be tiled, attach the ceramic edging first. Start with the "key" tile and make sure that the tiles on the work surface align exactly with those of the edging.

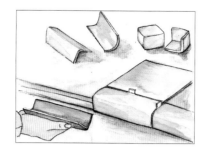

Spread adhesive over the work surface with a notched spreader. Do enough for about six tiles at a time.

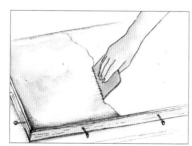

Lay all of the whole tiles in place, separating them with spacers. Do not forget to put spacers between the tiles and the edging.

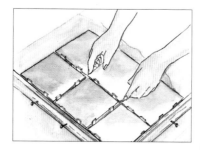

Press each row of tiles with a batten to ensure that they are level – check with a spirit level. Lift and relay wherever necessary – do not try to force the tiles into position.

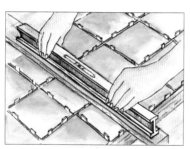

TILING AWKWARD AREAS

Tile the work surface before the splashback. Tile right up to the wall and then allow the wall tiles to overlap those at the edge of the countertop.

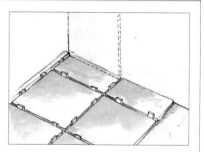

Curved tiles can be used for a neat join between the wall and countertop.

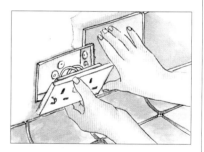

Remove socket faceplates and trim the tile to fit the hole. Put the faceplate back in place after grouting.

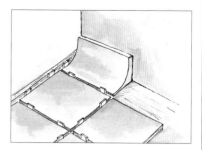

Take out burners (hobs) and tile under the edges. Do not forget to switch off the power when doing this. Use wooden battens to support them until you have finished grouting.

Overlap tiles at outside edges in the least noticeable way. Usually, the horizontal tiles overlap the vertical ones.

If you are starting from scratch, for the base use a good-quality plywood or blockboard at least ½in (12mm) thick, or ¾in (19mm) chipboard. Both must be supported along the edges about every 24in (600mm) – try to relate the size of the boards to the module of the tiles. Before you position the board on the top of the unit, cut holes to accommodate the appliances, sink, etc.

The edges of equipment may overlap the tiled surface, which will involve some loosening, etc. This may also be necessary when fitting tiles around power sockets and switches (always make sure the electricity supply is turned off at the fuse box).

Back to the Drawing Board

If you are planning a kitchen from scratch, you need to figure out exactly where everything is to be sited. Consider the basic principles of kitchen planning and fit in the "work triangle" in the most practical and convenient way. Also think of safety aspects – do not position the sink

▶ Work surface tiles do not have to be laid at right angles to the edges of units or walls. Here, the tiles are laid diamond-fashion to create extra visual interest. Take care to ensure that the grout lines look right on the countertop where they meet the wall tiles. [Country Floors]

FINDING THE MIDPOINT FOR A SPLASHBACK

Divide the length of the wall in two and use the edge of a tile as the midpoint.

Alternatively, it may look better to use the middle of a tile as the midpoint.

---

directly opposite the stove, or place the stove directly behind doors; it can also be dangerous to site the burners (hob) under a window.

When planning the layout of the work surface, it is best to make a scale plan to figure out exactly where the tiles and cuts will fall, and also to help you site the sink and other appliances. Use squared paper, making one tile equal to one or more squares – you can use squared paper even if the tiles are rectangular in shape. Aim for any cuts to be placed to the back of the units, and in the case of an L-shaped arrangement, make sure a whole tile meets its partner at the inner bend of the L, and that the joins are continuous along both surfaces.

Once you have the basic plan on paper, you can take it to the tile supplier and use it as a guide to purchase the right quantities. As with all tiling jobs, buy a few spare tiles to allow for mistakes!

Installing and Finishing

The method of installing tiles on a work surface is similar to that of wall or floor tiles. With the top in position, lay the tiles on the surface to make sure the plan is the most practical one. By doing this, a "key" tile will become evident, which is usually either centered on the surface or where the two extensions of the "L" meet. Draw around this tile on the surface to be tiled and use it as a guideline.

If you have opted for a ceramic tiled edge, install these tiles first; then work back towards the wall and sides with the main tiles, using the "key" tile as a guide. When tiling an edge, spread the adhesive on the back of the tile, not on the prepared surface. If you plan a wooden trim, this will be added later, but in the meantime, tack a piece of batten the same size as the trim along the edge of the work surface as a guide.

To tile the main area of the top, use a special notched spreader to spread enough adhesive to lay four to six tiles, ⅛in (2–3mm) thick. Push the tiles firmly into position, inserting spacers in between. Every so often, use a spirit level to check that the tiles are perfectly flush and level. Use a piece of batten to press the tiles down flat after laying an area of about four to six tiles, and if necessary, lift any which are standing out and relay them.

When the main tiles are laid, cut and lay any for the corners, for under the lip of inset fittings, or along the sides or back of the top. Lay upstanding edge tiles and any splashback tiles to be in line with the tiles on the work surface.

Clean the tiles and leave to harden for approximately 12–24 hours, and then apply the grout. Epoxy grout is sticky and different from conventional grout, and needs to be applied with a special applicator, following the manufacturer's instructions carefully.

SUPPLIERS

American Olean
75–02 88th Street
Glendale
New York
718 894 3200

Avarino Tile and Marble
1023 65th Street
Brooklyn
New York
718 680 0628

Cancos Tile Westbury Corp
801 Old Country Road
Westbury
New York
516 334 5700

Ceramica Arnon
134 West 20th Street
New York
212 807 0876

Charles Tiles
801 Light Street
Baltimore
Maryland
410 332 1500

Country Floors
8735 Melrose Avenue
Los Angeles
California
310 657 0510

Country Floors
15 East 16th Street
New York
212 627 8300

Crossville Tiles
Industrial Parkway
Crossville
Tennessee
615 456 3909

Demuth Handpainted Tiles
1758 Industrial Way
Napa
California
707 252 0544

Design Tile Inc
8455 B Tyco Road
Vienna
Virginia
703 734 8211

Elmax Lumber
1624 Webster Avenue
The Bronx
New York
718 299 1785

Elon Ltd
5 Skyline Drive
Hawthorn
New York
914 347 7800

**Empire State Marble
Manufacturing Corp**
207 East 110th Street
New York
212 534 2307

Facings of America
4121 North 27th Street
Phoenix
Arizona
602 955 9217

**Florida Tile Ceramic
Center**
305 West 2880 South
Salt Lake City
Utah
801 485 2900

Fuda Tile Inc
261 Route 46
Elmwood Park
New Jersey
New York
212 935 0810

Gen-Tile
1047 East Gunhill Road
The Bronx
New York
914 776 1731

Giurdanella Brothers
434 East 11th Street
New York
212 674 2097

**Grand Metro Home
Centers**
2524 Broadway
New York
212 749 4140

Hamilton Parker
165 West Vine Street
Columbus
Ohio
614 341 2314

Hastings
230 Park Avenue South
New York
212 674 9700

Ideal Tiles
2048 Broadway
70th Street
New York
212 799 3600

Jasba Tiles
1412 East Katella Avenue
Anaheim
California
714 938 0166

Latico
2943 Glenden Street
Los Angeles
California
213 664 1171

**D Marino Tile
Company**
444 Graham Avenue
Brooklyn
New York
718 389 2191

The Meredith Collection
PO Box 8854
Canton
Ohio
216 484 1656

Mondial Tiles
6501 14th Avenue
Brooklyn
New York
718 232 0800

Nemo Tile
48 East 21st Street
New York
212 674 9700

**Oak Leaf
Conservatories**
876 Davis Drive
Atlanta
Georgia
(US) 800 360 6283

**Quarry Tile Marble
and Granite**
192 Lexington Avenue
New York
212 679 8889

Quemere International
112 Franklin Avenue
Yonkers
New York
914 476 5950

**Sabo Tile and
Marble**
660 Saw Mill River Road
Yonkers
New York
914 376 3653

Ann Sacks
5 East 16th Street
New York
212 463 0492

Shelly
979 Third Avenue
New York
212 832 2255

Sonoma Tiles
7750 Bell Road
Windsor
California
707 837 8177

Standard Tile
255 Route 46 West
Totowa
New Jersey
New York
201 256 6412

Stanley Tile and Marble
136 East 28th Street
New York
212 685 8227

Status Tiles
107 West Denny Way
Seattle
Washington
206 282 0181

Stone Source Design Supply
215 Park Avenue South
New York
212 505 0009

Sunny McLean & Co
3800 NE 2nd Avenue
Miami
Florida
305 573 5943

Sun Tile
PO Drawer C
Estancia
New Mexico
800 552 1913

Tile Craft
Show Place Square East
135 Road Island Street
San Francisco
California
415 552 1913

Traditions in Tiles
351 Peach Tree Hills Avenue
Suite 140
Atlanta
Georgia
404 239 9186

**Ventimiglia and Piazza Artistic
   Marble and Tiles Works**
80–21 Myrtle Avenue

Glendale
New York
212 925 6141

WD Virtue Co Inc
PO Box 126
160 Broad Street
Summit
New Jersey
New York
908 273 6936

Walker Zanger
8901 Bradley Avenue
California
818 504 0235

**Westchester Tile and
   Marble Corp**
170 Brook Street (Rte 22)
Scarsdale
New York
914 725 4355

EUROPEAN SUPPLIERS

Baauw BV
Havenstraat 25
3131 BD Vlaardingen
(Netherlands) 104 34 32 55

Carreaux de Casbah
20 Wellington Lane
Montpelier
Bristol
(UK) 01179 427318

Ceramica Vogue
Direzione E Uffici
Via Alessandrina 45
20095 Cusano Milanino
(Italy) 02 66 42 21

Ceramica Bardelli
Via Pascoli, 4/6
20010 Vittuone
Milano
(Italy) 02-90111030

Corres Mexican Tiles
29 Great Suffolk Road

London
(UK) 0171 261 0941

Decorum Ceramic Studio
North's Estate
Piddington
High Wycombe
Bucks
(UK) 01494 882299

Elon Tiles
66 Fulham Road
London
(UK) 0171 460 4600

Fired Earth
Twyford Mill
Oxford Road
Adderbury
(UK) 01295 812088

H&R Johnson
Highgate Tile Works
Tunstall
Stoke-on-Trent
(UK) 01782 575575

Interlignes
20 rue de Chaligny
75012 Paris
(France) 43 07 37 14

Jones's Tiles
Orleton Manor
Ludlow
Shropshire
(UK) 01568 85666

Mosaic Workshop
Unit B
443–449 Holloway Road
London
(UK) 0171 263 2997

Paris Ceramics
386 King's Road
Chelsea
London
(UK) 0171 351 3467

Porcelanosa
Apdp Correos 131

12540 Villarreal
Castellon
(Spain) 964 52 12 62

Rye Tiles
The Old Brewery
Wishyard
Rye
Sussex
(UK) 01797 223038

Sally Anderson Ceramics
Parndon Mill
Harlow
Essex
(UK) 01279 420982

Société Carré
9 rue de Pierre
   de Geyter
Pierrefitte 93380
France
(France) 48 26 22 63

Tiles of Stow
Lanston Priory Workshops
Station Road
Kingham
Oxon
(UK) 01608 658951

Winchester Tile Company
Unit C1
Pegasus Court
Ardglen Road
Whitchurch
Hampshire
(UK) 01256 896922

World's End Tiles
BR Yard
Silverthorne Road
Battersea
London
(UK) 0171 720 8358

Mary Rose Young
Oak House
Arthur's Folly
Parkend, Lydney
Gloucestershire
(UK) 01594 563425

GLOSSARY

Accent colors: small amounts of color introduced to add interest or balance to a scheme.

Advancing colors: "warm colors in the spectrum which appear to come forward, making a space seem more cozy, but smaller.

Border tiles: narrow strips of material used to decorate or edge a wall area; usually curved and may have a raised design and protrude like a nosing; used above a part-tiled wall or dado to finish.

Carrés: literally "squares;" name given to natural terracotta slabs, usually from the Mediterranean.

Ceramic: a heat-resistant material made by firing or baking clay.

Chair rail: see Dado rail.

Clay: natural product taken from the earth and fired in kilns (or sometimes sunbaked) to make tiles; can be colored (red or earth tones) or white (china); for terra clay see Earthenware.

Color values: weight or strength of color, sometimes called tone.

Complementary colors: contrasting "opposite" colors; those which face each other on the color wheel; create a stimulating effect.

Crackle glaze: when characteristic imperfections in the glaze produce an "antique" effect; such tiles should not be used on work surfaces or shower walls where an impervious surface is required.

Dado: lower area of wall between dado rail and baseboard (skirting); traditionally wood-paneled or covered with heavily textured wallcovering and painted; may be tiled to provide a practical surface to withstand knocks.

Dado rail: also called a chair rail; a wooden beading or plaster molding mounted about 3ft (90cm) from the floor; can also be tiled; originally devised to prevent the backs of chairs from damaging fabric-hung walls; provides a convenient boundary between different wall treatments.

Drop-ins: small tiles which are combined with larger tiles to form a geometric pattern; mostly found in floor tiles; see Insets.

Earthenware: a type of coarse clay used for tiles and pottery.

Encaustic tiles: from the Greek for "burnt in;" an ancient method of producing inlaid tiles used in medieval monasteries and churches; the inlay process permanently fuses the pattern into the tile; characteristic colors are terracotta/black/beige (sometimes accented in blue).

Faience (Fayence): tin-enameled earthenware made in Europe in 16th–18th centuries.

Field tiles: usually plain-colored or slightly textured tiles intended for the major wall or floor area, but can be combined with patterned insets.

Glaze: a vitrified coating which makes tiles non-porous; added in liquid form before firing; the heat of the kiln produces a high gloss, although different types, such as matte, are also common.

Insets: see Drop-ins; can also refer to borders or pictorial tiles set into a plain floor or wall of field tiles.

Liner tiles: see Border tiles.

Luster: rich, fluid, iridescent sheen on the surface of some wall tiles which looks like an oilslick; created by mixing a thin film made from metallic salts with the glaze.

Majolica: a process where a slip of white clay applied to the surface of a tile highlights the colored glaze used in the final decoration; brought to Italy by Majorcan sailors c.1400.

Mosaics: small pieces of fired clay, glass or marble used to make a decorative pattern for floors and walls.

Motif: the dominant feature in a design, usually repeated regularly.

Mural: a picture or panel made from a combination of tiles.

Nosing: a type of border tile used to finish an area of tiling; often stands out in relief.

Onglaze: a method of glazing a predecorated tile with clear glaze so the pattern shows through.

Picture rail: simple beading running around walls below the cornice; pictures can be suspended by means of hooks and wires.

Receding colors: colors from the "cool" end of the spectrum, which appear to go away into the distance, so creating an impression of space.

Relief tiles: tiles with a raised design, creating a 3D effect, usually made by using a mold.

Repeat: full length of a vertical design taken from one point to the next point where it repeats itself exactly; single tiles can form a repeat, although geometric patterns usually rely on several tiles.

Silk-screen printing: a method of producing a pattern by squeezing glaze, dye or pigment through an etched screen onto the surface.

Slate: a type of natural quarried material suitable for indoor and outdoor use; often riven (roughened) to make it non-slip.

Slipware: made by combining clay with water; more usually white clay and water mixed to the consistency of cream, used to cover red clay to enhance and highlight the final decoration.

Stoneware: made by combining clay with flint or silica to produce a material which can withstand very high firing temperatures, creating tiles suitable for exterior use in intense weather conditions.

Terracotta: from the Latin meaning "fired earth;" normally used to describe unglazed earthenware – a low-fired red clay used for tiles and pottery; also used to describe a deep burnt-orange (natural clay) color.

Tesserae: individual units in a tesselated pavement; also used for geometric patterned tiles.

Tesselated pavement: floor made of hard-wearing mosaics set into a pattern – usually pictorial.

Tin glaze: glaze created by adding tin oxide to a lead glaze to produce a white opaque effect when fired.

Tint: a pale value of a color made by adding white to a pure hue.

Tone: a middle value or color made by adding gray to a pure hue.

Trompe l'oeil: literally to "deceive the eye;" method used to create a 3D effect on a flat plane or to simulate a view on a blank area of wall.

INDEX

Page numbers in *italics* refer to captions and illustrations

CREDITS

Quarto would like to thank all the tile manufacturers and retailers who so kindly supplied tiles and transparencies for use in this book.

We would also like to thank the following New York showrooms for allowing us to photograph many of their tiles: Ann Sacks, Country Floors, Elon Ltd, Ideal Tiles and Shelly.

We would particularly like to thank Mary Rose Young and Ann Sacks for their kind assistance and cooperation throughout the production of this book.

Jacket: Tiles supplied by Fired Earth; room photographs supplied by Bathing Beauties, London.

Suppliers of all tiles and photographs used in this book are indicated at the end of their accompanying captions except in the following cases.

a above; *m* middle (row); *b* below; *l* left; *r* right; *c* center

1 Mosaic Workshop / **2–3** Mosaic Workshop / **4–5** Mosaic Workshop / **8** Hastings *al, ac*; Country Floors *ar*; Ann Sacks *bl*; Fired Earth *br* / **9** Winchester Tile Company *al*; Country Floors *ar*; Hastings *bl*; Minton Hollins *bc*; Life Enhancing Tile Company *mr*; Mary Rose Young *br* / **13** Paris Ceramics / **19** Paris Ceramics / **27** H&R Johnson / **37** Sussex Terracotta / **45** H&R Johnson / **54–55** *Tiles for Color Directory section opener supplied by* Acquisitions Fireplaces, Bronwyn Williams-Ellis, Corres Mexican Tiles, Criterion Tiles, Elon, Hastings, Jaafar Design, Life Enhancing Tile Company, T&C Sloper Medieval Tiles, Marlborough Tiles, Mary Rose Young,

Reptile Tiles and Ceramics, Reject Tile Shop, Sally Anderson Ceramics, Sunny McLean & Co, Tower Ceramics Ltd, Tile with Style, Winchester Tile Company / **58–59** *Tiles for Red Directory opener supplied by* Country Floors, Criterion Tiles, Fired Earth, Marlborough Tiles, Mary Rose Young, Reject Tile Shop, Sunny McLean & Co, Tower Ceramics Ltd, The Tile Shop, Tile with Style, WD Virtue Co Inc, WT / **60** H&R Johnson *l*; Société Carré *r* / **61** Ann Sacks *l*; MS *r* / **70–71** *Tiles for Orange Directory opener supplied by* Bronwyn Williams-Ellis, Corres Mexican Tiles, Elon, Fired Earth, Life Enhancing Tile Company, T&C Sloper Medieval Tiles, Tower Ceramics Ltd, The Tile Shop, Sunny McLean & Co, Tile with Style / **72** Société Carré *l*; Colour 1 Ceramics *r* / **73** Bathing Beauties *a*; Corres Mexican Tiles *b* / **78** *Tiles for Yellow Directory opener supplied by* Bronwyn Williams-Ellis, Corres Mexican Tiles, Marlborough Tiles, Tile with Style, Winchester Tile Company / **80** Winchester Tile Company *l*; Paris Ceramics *r* / **81** Corres Mexican Tiles *l*; Mosaic Workshop *r* / **86–87** *Tiles for Green Directory opener supplied by* Acquisitions Fireplaces, Corres Mexican Tiles, Criterion Tiles, Elon, Jaafar Design, Life Enhancing Tile Company, Reject Tile Shop, Sally

Anderson Ceramics, Tile Art, Tower Ceramics Ltd, Tiles of Stow, Tile with Style, Winchester Tile Company / **88** H&R Johnson / **89** H&R Johnson *l*; Ann Sacks *ar*; Société Carré *br* / **97** Country Floors *al, acl, ml, bl, bc*; Shelly *acr, bcl*; Ann Sacks *ar, bcr, br*; Hastings *mc* / **98–99** *Tiles for Blue Directory opener supplied by* Bronwyn Williams-Ellis, Corres Mexican Tiles, Jaafar Design, Life Enhancing Tile Company, Steven Morgan, Marlborough Tiles, Reject Tile Shop, Sally Anderson Ceramics, Tiles of Stow, Tile with Style, Winchester Tile Company, WO / **100** H&R Johnson / **101** Fired Earth *l*; KA *ar*; Sally Anderson Ceramics *br* / **110–111** *Tiles for Neutral and Natural Directory opener supplied by* Corres Mexican Tiles, Elon, Life Enhancing Tile Company, Fired Earth, Reject Tile Shop, Sally Anderson Ceramics, Tower Ceramics Ltd, The Tile Shop / **112** Ann Sacks *l*; H&R Johnson *r* / **113** Ann Sacks *l, r* / **122–123** *Tiles for Black and White Directory opener supplied by* Elon, Fired Earth, Life Enhancing Tile Company, Mosaic Workshop, Quemere International, Reject Tile Shop, Tiles and Flooring, Tower Ceramics Ltd, Tiles of Stow, Tile with Style, Winchester Tile Company / **124** Topps Tile Kingdom *l*; Ann Sacks *r* / **125** Country Floors *l*; Ann Sacks *r* / **132** *Tiles for Metallic Directory opener supplied by* Country Floors, Hastings, Jones's Tiles, Mary Rose Young, Sunny McLean & Co, The Tile Shop, WD Virtue Co Inc / **133** Ann Sacks *l, r* / **136–137** *Tiles for Practical Pointers opener supplied by* Fired Earth, Life Enhancing Tile Company; *Tools supplied by* Tower Ceramics Ltd / **160** Mosaic Workshop

All other photographs are the copyright of Quarto.